"If She Weren't My Best Friend, I'd Kill Her!"

ALSO BY MERRY BLOCH JONES

"Please Don't Kiss Me at the Bus Stop!"
(Andrews McMeel Publishing, 1997)

"I Love Her, But . . ." (Workman, 1996)

"I Love Him, But . . ." (Workman, 1995)

*Birthmothers: Women Who Relinquished Babies for
Adoption* (Chicago Review Press, 1993)

*Stepmothers: Keeping It Together with Your Husband
and His Kids* (Birch Lane Press, 1992)

"If She Weren't My Best Friend, I'd Kill Her!"

Almost 600 Ways Women Drive Their Girlfriends Crazy

Merry Bloch Jones

Andrews McMeel Publishing
Kansas City

For information, write Andrews McMeel Publishing, an Andrews McMeel Universal company,
4520 Main Street, Kansas City, Missouri 64111.

www.andrewsmcmeel.com

Library of Congress Cataloging-in-Publication Data

If she weren't my best friend, I'd kill her! : Almost 600 ways women drive their girlfriends crazy /
[compiled by] Merry Bloch Jones.
      p.   cm.
   ISBN 0-8362-5276-4 (ppb)
   1. Friendship—Quotations, maxims, etc. 2. Women—Quotations,
maxims, etc. 3. Friendship—Humor. 4. Women—Humor. I. Jones,
Merry Bloch.
PN6084.F8I47   1998
177'.62—dc21   97-43283
                                                                          CIP

ATTENTION: SCHOOLS AND BUSINESSES

Andrews McMeel books are available at quantity discounts with bulk purchase for educational,
business, or sales promotional use. For information, please write to: Special Sales Department,
Andrews McMeel Publishing, 4520 Main Street, Kansas City, Missouri 64111.

To Robin, Baille, and Neely

ACKNOWLEDGMENTS

The late Connie Clausen represented five of my books and, despite her fragile health, consistently encouraged, energized, and supported my work. I will miss her sharp wit, tireless spirit, and unflinching honesty. The material in this book originated from research I did for *Glamour* magazine; thanks to Laura Matthews and Amanda Gordon there. Thanks also to agent Stedman Mays; to editors Chris Schillig and Nora Donaghy; to Susan Stone, Ileana Stevens, Gigi Campanelli, Karen Greenfield, Sue Small, Lanie Zera, Nancy Delman, Jane Braun, and the many other women all over the country who contributed comments with candor and enthusiasm, and, as always, to my mom, sister, and Robin, Baille, and Neely.

CONTENTS

GIRLFRIENDS

"If She Weren't My Best Friend, I'd Kill Her!"

I was complaining to my husband about a friend I'll call Lois. "Lois has nothing good to say about anyone," I said. "She calls me to complain about Marilyn. She probably calls Marilyn to complain about me—"

"So why do you spend half the day on the phone with her?" My husband has a limited capacity for commiseration. "If she upsets you so much, don't have anything to do with her."

"Don't be ridiculous," I snapped. As usual, he didn't get it.

"What's ridiculous about dropping someone who's continuously on your nerves?"

"I can't just *drop* her!" He could be so *simple*. "She's one of my best *friends*."

I thought the conversation was over and began to walk out of the room. But he wasn't finished. As I neared the door, I heard him sigh, "Women." He said it as if it were a final, conclusive statement. "Women," all of us, as if we were one and the same and equally confounding.

"What's *that* supposed to mean?"

"Nothing." He stared into his automobile magazine.

"Something. What?"

"Well, you say you're friends with Lois. But you really can't stand her. And, apparently, she can't stand anyone. So where does the *friend* part come in?"

"So, that's Lois. It's not all 'women.'"

"Fine. But every day you have another complaint. This one doesn't call you back, that one brags too much, the other one's too jealous. You call yourselves 'friends,' but I don't get it. I always thought 'friends' were supposed to *like* each other."

I stared at him, flabbergasted. The subtle textures and paradoxical complexities of the female psyche completely eluded him. Nonetheless, he had a point. Although Lois and I were close, we didn't necessarily *like* each other. We were friends because, well, we were friends. We lived in the same neighborhood, saw each other all the time. Knew people in common. Worked on the same committees at the school. Took our kids to the same after-school activities. It wasn't about *liking*, really. It was about convenience, expedience, being at the same place at the same time, sharing common experiences and frustrations. And needing female companionship.

And besides, I told myself, not all my friendships were like the one with Lois. Some had survived from childhood, passed tests of time and distance, endured marriages, divorces, moves, careers, and parenthood. I liked most of my friends a lot. A real lot.

But, even though I could defend certain of my friendships, my husband's comments disturbed me. I began to think about women's friendships in general, the range of feelings they involve, the simultaneous pulls and pushes, irritations and affections, conceits and concerns. And I began to wonder if I were unusual. Did other women weave friendships with simpler, less twisted thread? Or was ambivalence inherent to the very fiber of female friendship?

Answering these questions led to this book. In it, some four hundred women, aged twenty-one and up, located all over the country, tell us not only that, yes, their best friends bug them, but also precisely when, where, and how.

The friendships they refer to are at least five years old. Most of these women have attended college; many hold graduate degrees. Among them are stay-at-home moms, doctors, nurses, dental and medical technicians, a dentist, an accountant, writers, account executives, teachers, an interior decorator, a landscape architect, hairdressers, public relations consultants, market researchers, hospital administrators, bank officers, retailers, sales reps, editors, actresses, real estate agents, a policewoman, a dietician, psychologists, social workers, waitresses, fund-raisers, secretaries, scientists, computer programmers, and a newscaster.

Their answers were gathered by phone, fax, mail, and e-mail; contacts were made through an informal network of family and friends and the family and friends of family and friends across the country; through contributors to my former books; through chance meetings on airplanes or in markets and malls, and through various national and community organizations.

Gathering these comments, I realized that the very definition of "girlfriend" is hazy; women's friendships take many forms.

We seek solace from one friend, stimulation from another. We make mischief with one, meditate with another. In each relationship, we take on somewhat different roles, playing, at various times, the shrink or the shrunk, the darer or the dared, mother or child, princess or peasant, leader or led. If we feel perky on a given day, we may avoid a quiet pal in favor of a compatibly perky person. If not, we may not. Or we may, to perk us up.

Depending on our mutual momentary moods, we may or may not be in harmony with our best, closest friends. Our friendships sustain us, but are nevertheless subject to tides and timing, and are often fraught with conflicts and contradictions.

On these pages, with wry humor and relentless candor, women around the country let us into their private lives and relationships. Their compiled comments create an unadorned portrait of American women's friendships in the context of everyday, real life. And, as you will see, they have no shortage of complaints. Friends annoy, provoke, control, and embarrass each other on a daily basis. But while their actions generate complaints, they also create a testament to the strength, importance, and depth of their friendships. Their bonds are vital enough that women endure the irritating and the outrageous for friendship's sake. Their humor is wry enough to keep the downside of their relationships in perspective. And their connections are deep enough to survive the aggravation they get from and give to each other over the course of time.

Whatever bugs them about their buddies, with all their gripes and complaints, the women in this book hang in there. The positives outweigh the negatives so that, as time goes on, their friendships survive. And sometimes flourish.

All the same, I'm ready to kill Lois.

CHAPTER 1

MIRRORS

"If She Weren't My Best Friend, I'd Kill Her!"

Intentionally or not, women friends help define each other. Modeling, mimicking, mothering, or smothering, we act as mutual sounding boards, trading feedback and advice as only females can. On a daily basis, we confide, conspire, commiserate, and compare, relying upon each other for companionship and support.

Even so, many friends find that closer is not always better. When borders become blurred, friends can be crunched by too much contact.

"She has the keys to my apartment," says Marly, 28. "I find her there when I come home from work, munching my pretzels, drinking my tea. Sometimes, she's even wearing my clothes—stuff she might or might not return."

Given borders and breathing room, though, our interfemale friendships can help us see ourselves as the people we want or need to be. By association, contagion, or comparison, friends make us feel good about ourselves. In their company, we become stimulating, smart, successful, pretty, or popular. So that, whether we seek celebrity or security, wisdom or whimsy, when we look at our female pals, we often get a clearer view of ourselves. Which can be real annoying.

She comes into the john with me. I'm going to the bathroom, and she's talking, commenting on whatever. If I get in fast enough to lock her out, she'll knock, and then stand outside talking through the door.

Marilyn, 26, Pittsburgh, Pa.

She's always touching, standing on top of you. The woman has no idea of personal space. When she stands next to you, you feel her breath on your face. You know what she's had to eat that day. She hugs you, smashes herself against your boobs. She puts her hands on my face, grabs my arm, taps my shoulders, strokes my hair. I love her, but I'm always backing away, out of reach. Especially in the summer.

Renee, 29, Rochester, N.Y.

I dodge, but she greets me with a big wet kiss. I don't mind the lipstick marks so much. Or her breasts crushing mine. It's her saliva on my face. *That* gets me.

Yvonne, 41, Bronxville, N.Y.

11

When she had her nose done, she took my picture to the plastic surgeon and said, "I want one like hers." She dyes her hair my color, wears heels to be my height. I suppose it's flattering.

Carson, 23, Tulsa, Okla.

Whatever I do, Lorrie copies me. I get a second hole in my ears; she gets hers pierced, too. I get my hair cut; she gets hers cut. I get a new car; she gets a new car. I get engaged; she gets engaged. I had my first child in August; she had hers five weeks later. It's fascinating. I'm waiting to see what she'll do now that I'm getting a divorce.

Rhonda, 33, New York, N.Y.

If I like something Lauren doesn't, she actually gets mad. She was furious that I liked the movie *The Piano*. She took it as a personal insult and argued, tried to change my mind for days. Weeks. If the subject came up today, she'd argue with me again.

Pam, 52, Fort Worth, Tex.

She forgets what she's going to say in the middle of a sentence. She calls to tell me something and then she can't remember what it was. So I start talking about something else. All of a sudden, she remembers why she called and interrupts to tell me. When she's finished, I can't remember what *I* was talking about. And neither can she.

Eva, 53, Phoenix, Ariz.

13

She treats her opinions as fact. She will not brook any contradictions or disagreements. If you state another point of view, she's speechless. Stunned. Personally betrayed.

Paula, 28, Chicago, Ill.

She calls me all day long. Four times yesterday. First, to tell me that they'd sold out of the chicken special at the market. Next, that her mom has cataracts. Then to say that it's supposed to rain Thursday, maybe thunderstorms. And then to say she forgot to tell me that, even though the chicken's gone, they have a great price on turkey breast.

Terri, 33, St. Louis, Mo.

eg makes a big deal about confiding. Makes you swear not to repeat what she's telling you. Then, she tells you the same story she told you three days ago. I have to wonder, if the story's so confidential, why doesn't she remember telling it? I suspect that she tells everyone she knows the same stuff, and she says it's "secret" so we'll feel special.

Corky, 40, Enid, Okla.

She cannot tolerate silence. She'll say anything, just to keep the patter going. She'd recite the alphabet rather than have quiet.

Dierdre, 41, New Orleans, La.

She knows my past and delights in publicly recounting everything embarrassing I've ever done. She thinks it's great cocktail conversation to tell how I passed out drunk in the dorm elevator and rode up and down all night with people stepping over me to get in and out. She loves to tell how when I was her maid of honor, my filet flew across the dinner table. Well, it's not my fault. The meat was tough and the knife was dull.

JoEllyn, 26, Davenport, Iowa

Joanne gossips. She tells me awful things about people. About her friends, her sisters. Even her husband. So I worry sometimes. If she talks to *me* about *them,* what does she talk to *them* about?

Sydney, 27, Providence, R.I.

17

T. J. says, "I don't have a mean bone in my body." She really believes this about herself, even while she's dissecting people and dicing their characters to mincemeat.

Sally, 32, Raleigh, N.C.

Kate interviews me. She asks details of every place I've been, every job I've had, every relationship I've had, every guy I've dated. She hangs on every word, as if she'll be tested. It's flattering to fascinate someone so much, but it makes me nervous. Like, why does she need to know all this? Is she writing a résumé? Planning to be my understudy? Preparing to assume my personality?

Olivia, 44, Orlando, Fla.

She corrects my speech. "Not 'me,' Lorraine. 'I.'"

Lorraine, 39, Winnetka, Ill.

There is no subject she won't discuss, nothing's too personal. But she chooses the worst times for her topics. She insisted on discussing female orgasms, in detail, just after my engagement was broken. Sex was not my favorite topic then. When I was desperate to get pregnant, she went on about how ineffective birth control was for her, how fertile she was. How she got pregnant every time her husband looked at her. Right before my first child was born, she wanted to tell me labor horror stories. I stopped her, so she talked instead about the ugly stretch marks some women get.

Joyce, 39, Denver, Colo.

19

I can't lie to her. She catches me every time, makes me 'fess up. I can't even exaggerate. She catches me more often than my mom does. She looks me in the eye and says, "Shawna, you're busted."

Shawna, 22, Marion, Ohio

Irene tells me how to live my life. "Sell your house, dye your hair, get a face-lift, stop eating meat, join my tennis club." Whatever I do by myself is wrong or misled. I can't get a tooth filled without her insisting, "You should have used the toothpaste I told you about; you wouldn't have had a cavity."

Lindsey, 39, Villanova, Pa.

Barb talks about celebrities as if they're in our social circle, as if we know them personally. If I talk about a problem I'm having, she'll say, "Well, think about what happened to Whitney Houston," or Elizabeth Taylor, Princess Diana, Bill Cosby. Someone we don't know and never will. To her, something she read in the paper seems just as real and important as our own real lives.

Jessica, 31, Skokie, Ill.

Myra can't stand to be alone. Even when she's driving, she needs company. If she can't get me to go with her, she calls from the car.

Jacquie, 44, Stamford, Conn.

If I don't pick up, Renee talks to my phone machine. My husband and I are having sex, and there's Renee's nasal soprano in the next room, detailing her daughter's allergy symptoms or repeating an argument with her ex.

Lisa, 39, Ft. Worth, Tex.

22

There's no such thing as a short conversation with Jess. When she calls, I'm stuck for an hour, at least.

Elana, 38, Glenside, Pa.

Flo makes me chicken soup when I'm sick. Bakes cakes not just for my birthday, but to celebrate anything—new shoes, clean closets, a rainy day— anything. When I'm depressed, she comes over and washes my dishes, makes my bed. Trims my philodendron. The woman needs someone to take care of. She means well, but I wish she'd get a boyfriend, or at least a dog.

Phyllis, 32, Phoenix, Ariz.

She calls me and talks to her children. I hold on while she tells them to stop fighting or watching TV, to start doing their homework, stop throwing balls in the dining room, take the dog out, or take baths. She must never talk to them except when she has me on the phone.

Opal, 37, Darby, Pa.

Louise says everything in one sentence. One long, winding, run-on, unpunctuated, endless sentence. If you want to enter the conversation, you have to jump in, real loud, between phrases. I swear, the woman can inhale while she's talking, because I've never caught her taking a breath.

24

Reggie, 47, Elgin, Ill.

Rita calls me every day at 7:15 A.M., no exceptions, to give me the weather report and discuss what we're wearing to work.

Mindy, 30, Austin, Tex.

I can never repay her. She's been there for me when my grandmom died; when Craig, my boyfriend for eight years, dumped me; when I totaled my mom's Camaro. Whenever I've been in a mess, she's helped me get through it. I'm forever indebted. If I started today and worked for ten years, I'd probably never make it up to her. And, believe me, she likes it that way.

Tina, 24, Philadelphia, Pa.

25

She calls me from her car to complain about traffic.

Melody, 30, Detroit, Mich.

She uses the word "we," as if we're the same person. "Remember all the guys *we* went out with? The stunts *we* pulled? Remember going with Paul, cheating on him with his best friend, Eric, sneaking out the window and drinking beer all night, stealing the answers to the physics exam, trying to act straight so our parents wouldn't know we were stoned?" I don't remember doing this stuff. But in her mind, if she did it, I was there, too. She insists on this.

Crystal, 37, Denver, Colo.

She talks on the phone all day long. Does not stop for anything. You hear her run the vacuum, chew her food, splash the bathwater. You hear paper rustling and the toilet flush. The girl would rather talk on the phone than have sex, and you'd probably hear that, too, if you listened.

Yvonne, 22, Chicago, Ill.

She reads the paper and worries. Every day, she has some new item that we can do nothing about but fret over. She was distraught for days because the polar ice caps might be melting. And *don't* mention the ozone layer in her presence.

Gwen, 29, Atlanta, Ga.

27

Roz gives me stacks of books and magazine articles to read. Then she asks my opinion of the content, the writing, the viewpoint. She quizzes me.

Susan, 34, Minneapolis, Minn.

She sends me cards. Cards for birthdays, for Christmas, for Easter. Cards if I'm sick. Cards if we've argued. Friendship cards. Cards that she thinks are funny, wicked, wry, or that have scantily clad, sexy hunks on the front. PMS cards. Cards with cute dogs or cuddly babies. She keeps entire card companies in business.

Elaine, 24, Portland, Oreg.

Jean tells me she's going to dress casually and shows up dressed to the nines; I look like a frump in my jeans. Or, the opposite—she says an affair is semiformal but shows up in slacks and a sweater while I'm in a cocktail dress.

Darby, 23, Chicago, Ill.

andy lives by the motto: "Your closet is my closet; your refrigerator is my refrigerator." She never hesitates to take stock of what I have, borrow it, or eat it.

Melissa, 39, Alexandria, Va.

anie signs me up for things. Classes, theater tickets, tennis leagues, concert series. She assumes I'll go when and where she goes, like we're attached at the waist. If I have other plans, she's insulted. It's gotten to the point where I check with her to see if my calendar's clear before I make plans.

Kate, 31, St. Louis, Mo.

hloe borrows my stuff. It looks better on her. It also *smells* like her when she gives it back.

Jillian, 30, Highland Park, Ill.

know she's my best friend, but I'm not sure I'm hers. With women, it's not like with men. With a man, you know where you stand. You're sleeping with him or you're not. You're engaged or you're not. But women don't "go steady." We don't take vows. There's no public declaration of the relationship. Nobody throws a shower for "best friends." So I don't know if it's equal. And to ask her if I'm her best friend would be weird. Besides, it could change any time, so I'd have to keep asking, like every day.

Karen, 21, Norfolk, Conn.

31

She tells me I look great when I *know* I look like hell. Like when I've been up all night cleaning vomit off my son's sheets and have bags under my eyes, cowlicks in my hair, and a pimple on my nose. If that's *great,* what does she think I look like normally?

Marsha, 37, Yonkers, N.Y.

Everything's political to her. Getting your hair cut short is a feminist statement. Driving a Saab is a liberal statement. Diamonds, emeralds, and fur are fascist. Makeup is sexist. Commercial television is decadent. Every time you eat, buy, wear, or look at something, you're casting a political vote.

Dorothy, 44, Lansing, Mich.

She eats off my plate. We're out to lunch and she reaches her fork over and helps herself to a wad of potato salad or whatever. If I complain, she offers me a forkful of her food, shrugs, and says, "You can taste mine any time."

Aviva, 27, South Bend, Ind.

Ida never says you're wrong or judges anything. She says, "Friends don't 'should' on each other," and accepts whatever you say or do, however you feel, no matter how negative, no matter how bizarre. If you said you wanted to machine-gun the supermarket, she'd accept this and nod. She tolerates you even when you can't tolerate yourself. She's infuriating.

Dena, 43, Lexington, Ky.

33

Ava nags me to quit my job. She tries to make me feel guilty for not being a stay-at-home mom like she is, but I think she just wants me home so we can goof off and hang out like in the old days. Parenting's just an excuse.

Courtney, 33, New York, N.Y.

Kanikah believes that red meat is the cause of violent crime in our society. She suspects that chemicals used to spray crops lead to moral decay; they get into the food chain and lodge in various parts of our brains, or something. She grows herbs, mixes up "tonics," gives her kids "teas" to counteract the fluoride in their water. Scolds me if I mention meatloaf.

Jasmine, 29, Telluride, Colo.

Barb's reborn. She worries about my soul, tries to convert me. Tells me what will happen if I'm not saved. Fire, brimstone, melting eyeballs. The whole nine yards.

Kelly, 31, New Orleans, La.

35

If I get hot flashes, she's on the Internet, finding herbal treatments for menopause. If I get a rash, she's on the Internet, finding herbal treatments for skin allergies. She nags me to go to health stores for the herbs. When I told her she was really irritating me, she got right on the Internet, finding herbal treatments for irritability.

Mona, 48, Anaheim, Calif.

She tells me I'm wasting electricity and turns off my lights. She walks through the house, shutting off the radio, the TV, the coffeepot. Whatever's on. She leaves and there I am, in a dark, silent apartment. With cold coffee.

Peggy, 31, San Francisco, Calif.

Erika's a vegetarian, but not for health reasons. It's because she believes in reincarnation. I can't eat a cheeseburger or a pork chop without her wondering aloud if I'm chewing on Grandma Sylvia.

Andrea, 25, Ft. Wayne, Ind.

Maggie's jealous of my other friends. Whenever I spend time with anybody else, she gives me the third degree. "Where did you go, what did you eat, how late did you stay out, what did you talk about, did you make plans to get together again?" She's worse than my boyfriend. Worse than my mother. It's like she's petrified I'll like someone better than I like her.

Sophie, 25, Minneapolis, Minn.

She made a joke about how sad it is that we're not lesbians, that we'd make a perfect couple. Then she joked about how maybe we should try it someday; it can't be worse than men. When I told her that sex is the only *good* thing about men, she just looked at me.

Fran, 33, Wilmington, Del.

No matter what I do, no matter how outrageous, Sharon defends me. If I got caught red-handed, a smoking revolver in my hand, a dead body beside me, she'd insist it was purely a coincidence. She should be a lawyer. In high school, she actually convinced our Spanish teacher that just because my clothes smelled like tobacco and I was exhaling grey fumes, he shouldn't assume I was *smoking*.

Jane, 23, Ann Arbor, Mich.

OUR BODIES, OURSELVES

"If She Weren't My Best Friend, I'd Kill Her!"

Even if our friends remain constant, our bodies don't. Our friends witness our changes, whether intentional or merely inevitable. Our weights soar and plunge. We swell in pregnancy, sag postpartum. Our hair goes from long to short, puffy to sleek, quiet brown to dignified grey to flaming red. We shape our brows, straighten our teeth, stretch our hamstrings, struggle with our abs. We redo our noses, tighten our eyes, alter the shapes of our busts, butts, and thighs.

Eventually, most of us come to accept our bodies and learn that our true friends love us regardless of exteriors. They love us, yes. But they also have opinions. We can be sure that our appearances—however well accepted—do not go unnoticed, unevaluated, or uncritiqued by our friends. Those who know us best never fail to find each flaw and eye each imperfection.

Whatever they observe, though, we are reassured that our friends will always appreciate the timeless beauty of the people we are inside, underneath, within.

After all, they expect—and depend upon—the same from us.

We used to dress alike, wear identical outfits in high school. One Halloween, we were a pair of dice. We were like twins. So when did she begin to look fifteen years younger than I do, and weigh forty pounds less?

Kathy, 38, Boston, Mass.

Every time she passes a mirror, she poses. Puckers the lips, sticks out the chest. Fluffs the hair. Not that she's vain or anything.

Sally, 22, Phoenix, Ariz.

She'd look good without makeup in the middle of the night. Her skin has not one blemish or line. There are never dark circles under her eyes. She doesn't have a single spider vein, not one. Her sweat smells like lily of the valley. Her nails never break. Even her hair is perfect. She wears a size six. Actually, I don't know why I like this woman. There must be *something*.

Jean, 41, St. Cloud, Minn.

43

She's so beautiful that people—especially men—always want to do things for her. They can't do enough. Need a lift, Sheila? Can I get you anything while I'm at the market, Sheila? Can I change your tire, Sheila? Get you tickets to a show? Take you to Paris for a few weeks? Buy you a fur coat? An emerald ring? Men follow her, begging her to let them please her. Meantime, I can't get a waiter to refill my coffee. Of course, he'll bring Sheila dessert on the house.

Monica, 28, Bethesda, Md.

I'm half her height and twice her weight, but she complains to *me* that she's gained five pounds.

Marthe, 32, Baltimore, Md.

She's completely unaware of how sensual she is. Her lips caress her food. Her fingers massage the steering wheel or her coffee mug. She can make washing dishes look exotic—almost indecent. When she eats an apple, it's just about obscene. I've seen men drool watching her fill her gas tank.

Rachel, 36, Aspen, Colo.

She wears so much costume jewelry, she rattles when she moves. Even when she breathes. Her earrings are hard to describe. Huge birds, or papier-mâché animals with hoops around them. She has so many bangles it's hard to lift her hand.

Phoebe, 47, Miami, Fla.

Wanda has stood by me through pimples, I mean *bad* ones, and entire weeks of bad hair. Without flinching. She's my best friend. For life.

RoseMarie, 28, Aberdeen, S.Dak.

Sherry weighs herself thirty times a day. When she wakes up, after she exercises, eats, or bathes. Whenever she goes to the bathroom. If the scale shows a pound more than she expects, she insists that I weigh myself, too, to see if it's accurate. If I want to make her really nuts, I tell her the scale *is* off—it shows my weight as five pounds too *low*.

Jessica, 26, Tulsa, Okla.

She's obsessed with fitness, has to be exercising all the time. We'll be at a PTA meeting at the school, and she'll grin at me and whisper, "Guess which muscles I'm working right now? Do it with me." Then she'll half-close her eyes and count, "One and two and . . ." For the rest of the meeting.

Gwen, 34, Laramie, Wyo.

We walk every morning and she has an inch of green cream on her skin. I can't look at her. People stare. She says she saves time by doing her facial while we're out.

Cameron, 29, Montgomery, Ala.

No matter what we're talking about, she manages to relate it to herself. Not just to herself. Specifically, to the size of her nose. The national deficit? It's smaller. Overcrowded prisons? She could rent out space inside it. *That* would be hard time. Sex? Her nose is so big, she can only have it from behind. Why does she do this? Is she hoping someone'll say it isn't as big as she thinks it is? No one can say that. She's got a big nose. But, like, enough already. No one cares.

Midge, 38, Rockport, Maine

She wants everyone to know her red hair's real, so she doesn't shave her legs or underarms.

Debbie, 26, Dover, Del.

She's decided to "let the goddess emerge." That means no more rinsing away the grey. No cosmetics. No shaving. No struggling to maintain her figure. No censorship; she expresses what she thinks, no matter what. I'm having trouble with it, I really am.

Emma, 55, Milwaukee, Wis.

People call her "The Hat Lady." She has all shapes, sizes, vintages. A hat for every mood or whim. That's actually how I met her—she was in front of me on the bus and her hat brim kept whapping my face. That's how she meets most people. Not necessarily whapping them, but because of her hats. She's got pillboxes, feather numbers, bonnets, creations too showy for Carmen Miranda. Every fabric, shape, and color. She's always wearing them. In seven years, I've never seen the top of her head.

Clara, 57, New York, N.Y.

Let's just say that Queen Elizabeth has better taste in clothes than Tina.

Becky, 39, Boston, Mass.

She convinced me to join a health club so we could go get our bodies back in shape. But she won't go; she doesn't want anyone to see her body because it's not in shape.

Sarah, 34, Clearwater, Fla.

In all the years I've known her, I've never seen Vera's feet. She says they're always cold, wears socks all the time. She won't go swimming, wears sneakers to the ocean, says she can't stand to have wet sand between her toes. I suspect they're webbed. Or maybe there are six toes. It's got to be something like that.

Vivian, 57, Wilmington, Del.

For my birthday, she gave me a gift certificate for a tattoo. So we can get matching ones. Have matching body art. She wants me to get mine *first,* then she'll get hers. Right.

Tanya, 23, Cleveland, Ohio

She's decided to stop being subjected to traditional, male-dominated concepts of fashion and to "be herself." In other words, she's stopped shaving her legs and tweezing her facial hair. Now, all I think about when I look at her are chin hairs. They scream, "Pluck me! Pluck me!" I've got a tweezers somewhere in my pocketbook. It's all I can do to control myself.

Serena, 46, San Jose, Calif.

She takes her shoes off wherever she goes.
Then she can't find them. When we want to leave a
restaurant, she's under the table, searching.

Lillian, 30, Nyack, N.Y.

She sniffs me, asks if I'm wearing cologne. Or tells
me I should.

Antoinette, 24, New Orleans, La.

Alice is embarrassed about biological functions.
She goes to the bathroom only to "powder her nose,"
runs the water so you won't hear her pee.

Gretchen, 26, Ogden, Utah

She's into waxing. When she gets her legs waxed, it's all she talks about. "Feel my legs. They're *so* silky. I *love* rubbing my thighs together." And she says this no matter who's around. The gardeners. My husband. My fifteen-year-old son.

Sylvia, 39, Winnetka, Ill.

Everything about her body embarrasses her. The tiniest, most dainty burp makes her turn bright red. She even sneezes like a mouse, won't let it out.

Cecily, 24, Randolph, Vt.

She's having the silver taken out of her fillings; she's convinced she's getting mercury poisoning from them. She fasts, and takes an enema every day so she can cleanse her system. She gets some kind of holistic injections. And she pays someone a fortune to "massage her aura."

Lacey, 31, Tacoma, Wash.

55

Clarissa does not hold back about passing gas. She lets it rip, whenever, wherever. Doesn't matter who's there. She's tooted in public, at lunch tables, in lines at stores, in elevators, in front of her teenagers and their dates, in front of my seven- and five-year-olds. I'm trying to teach my kids to say, "Excuse me," when they pass gas, but there she is, an adult, humming a tune or having a conversation, blasting off without a word of apology. Everyone around her is blushing, holding their breath, gagging, giggling, running out of the room, but she's oblivious. She's just fine with it.

Ophelia, 40, Baltimore, Md.

Every so often, she decides that it's not healthy to bathe every day; it "interferes with the body's natural chemistry." If I comment on her odor, she shrugs and says, "Grow up, Helene. It's natural."

Helene, 43, Boulder, Colo.

She loves hearts. She collects them. Her clothes are covered with them, and her accessories include heart-shaped earrings, buttons, rings, lockets, charms. She also has hearts on her curtains, shower curtains, toilet paper, towels. She has heart-shaped pillows, soft sculptures, vases, lamps. Oh, I forgot the underwear.

Heather, 33, Atlanta, Ga.

She bites her nails. It makes me so nervous, I want to bite mine.

Sylvie, 38, Richmond, Va.

She's a chub. She shouldn't wear shorts or short skirts or bikinis. But she does, and *I'm* not going to tell her about her jelly rolls.

Amena, 33, Mobile, Ala.

She wears sweaters several times before washing them. We're talking ripe.

Ruth, 38, Lincoln, Nebr.

Darlene will not do anything remotely glitzy. No pizzazz. Grey and beige are her favorite colors. It took me twelve years to get her to pierce her ears, but all she'll wear are tiny opal studs. I bought her a red sweater; it went right back to the store, exchanged for taupe. I tell her to get with it. She tells me to get *#!ed. Actually, language is the most colorful thing about her.

Hallie, 27, Brooklyn, N.Y.

Her fingernails are so long that they curl around like they belong to the empress of China. Or a bird of prey.

Jade, 22, Chicago, Ill.

59

Sophie has seven earring holes on the left; four in the right. She dresses like a teenager. You can't convince her that she isn't one. She even likes their music, or claims to.

Trish, 41, Louisville, Ky.

Barbara will not get her hair wet. She doesn't go out on rainy days unless it's an absolute emergency, and then she'll wear one of those plastic bag things on her head. She never goes near a pool or the beach. Only professionals at the salon wash her hair; it's nothing she'd ever try at home.

Caroline, 63, Evanston, Ill.

If I wear a new outfit, she'll say, "Perfect. It's *you*." Or, "No. Doesn't work. Sorry, it's just not you." What the hell does she mean? What are the criteria for "me" or "not me"? She won't say. She just says, "Trust me."

Gayle, 30, Columbia, Mo.

If she lies, she turns beet red. Her chest and neck get blotchy. So, like, you can tell, when she says you look great and she loves your outfit, if you'd really better go home and change.

Sonia, 24, Phoenix, Ariz.

She uses those glue-on nails. Like anyone would think they were actual fingernails. They're mother-of-pearl colored. And at least one's always fallen off, exposing this pathetic, crusty, bludgeoned-looking fingertip.

MaryBeth, 21, South Bend, Ind.

Do *not* grab her by the hands. Her nails are so long, you'll get your wrists slashed.

Laurie, 31, Cambridge, Mass.

She picks at her cuticles. Or hangnails. Or broken fingernails. Or something. She's always messing with her fingertips. It's hard to get her attention.

Maggie, 23, Palo Alto, Calif.

She's started getting patterns painted on her nails. Her hair's dyed platinum. She's into the "hooker" look.

Claire, 50, Narberth, Pa.

Liz owns every shade of nail polish ever bottled. She spends hours painting her toes and fingers, can't ever do anything manual because her nails aren't "quite dry."

Amanda, 34, Montgomery, Ala.

Rita's heavily into her deep maroon phase. Everything's maroon, from her bras to her bedding— even her eye shadow's maroon. It's terrible, but it will pass. Six months ago, everything was lime green.

Pat, 27, Indianapolis, Ind.

Pink's her favorite color. Everything she has is pink. Unless it's purple.

Abbey, 37, Concord, N.H.

She always wears black. It looks like she wears the same outfit every day. If you mention this, she says, "It's basic. What else do I need?"

Dena, 34, Kansas City, Mo.

She wears bows in her hair. Every day, no matter where we're going. No matter what she's wearing. There's always a bow.

Rachel, 53, Overbrook, Pa.

65

The woman refuses to wear her glasses. She'll walk right past me without recognizing me. She'll bump into parking meters and say, "Excuse me." She'll put cayenne instead of cinnamon in the iced tea. But she will *not* wear her glasses.

Rebecca, 39, Meadowbrook, Pa.

She wears her hair the way she did in high school. A flip. A big bouffant flip.

Loreen, 42, Chattanooga, Tenn.

Her hair's purple. It used to be hennaed until it turned orange. Now, it's purple. What, can't she see it? What does it look like to her? I mean, does she look in the mirror?

Karen, 43, Nashville, Tenn.

She irons her hair to take the frizz out. Singes the ends. If I see her in the morning, I smell burnt hair.

Yvonne, 39, Dayton, Ohio

She has the worst broken ends. The woman's hair's been bleached till it's straw, but you can't talk to her about it. She thinks blonde's beautiful, and that's the end of it.

Marybelle, 37, Laredo, Tex.

She has a way of leaning back and thoughtfully scratching her head. I mean *scratching*. Deep, head-lice-type scratching. And then, while she's talking to you, she digs pieces of scalp skin out from under her fingernails. At least, you hope it's scalp skin.

April, 31, Pittsburgh, Pa.

No matter how hot it is, even though her air-conditioner doesn't work, she will not let you open the window of her car. It might mess her 'do.

Anne, 23, Reno, Nev.

Sometimes she'll let her roots grow out for, like, three inches. I don't know, maybe she's waiting for somebody to mention it.

Reggie, 31, Jacksonville, Fla.

Elyssa insists that she has no grey hair. Yeah, and my father was George Washington.

Kathy, 43, Cincinnati, Ohio

She paints a fake beauty mark on her cheek. Big black thing. Looks like it might crawl away.

Phyllis, 52, Atlantic City, N.J.

She's a dear, but she's goes heavy on the makeup. What's the name of that vampiress creature? Elvira?

Kimberly, 40, Corpus Christi, Tex.

Her makeup settles around the creases in her skin. How do you tell someone that she looks like her face is cracking?

Jen, 50, Evanston, Ill.

When I have PMS, she tolerates everything I say. She acts like I'm a raving lunatic. It's infuriating. If something bugs me, she says, "We'll talk about this next week." Like she's decided that I'm irrational and incapable of clear thinking because of my hormones. As if *she* isn't a complete psycho on certain days.

Monica, 26, Pueblo, Colo.

She turns the heat down when your teeth are chattering. Your hands freeze onto the silverware. You can't see because of your breath clouding the air. But she's got her hot flashes, can't cool off, so tough for the rest of us.

Debra, 47, Lansing, Mich.

71

She's always hot and I'm always cold. When we're together for any length of time, we have knock-down, drag-out fights about where to set the thermostat. In the car, I turn the car heater up; she turns it back down. I turn it back up; she turns it back down. I turn it up again, she opens the window. When I reach over to lock the windows shut, she goes for the heater.

Laurie, 52, St. Paul, Minn.

She has T-shirts that announce her moods. "Horny and Dangerous." Or, "Warning: PMS." Her favorite, I think, is "Psycho Bitch from Hell." I see that one a lot.

Fawn, 24, San Jose, Calif.

Laura taught me about tampons. She also explained how to get pregnant and how not to. She taught me more about sex than anyone. More than my mother. More than my doctor. *Certainly* more than my husband.

Antoinette, 29, Escondido, Calif.

She *must* drink her eight glasses of water a day, no matter what. If we're shopping, we have to stop at a restaurant and I have to order coffee or a muffin, because all she wants is a glass of water and a refill. And then, of course, we can't go anywhere or do anything because, five minutes after we leave, she's got to run to the bathroom.

Michelle, 43, Orlando, Fla.

She's always ovulating and announcing how fertile she is.

Cindy, 34, Little Rock, Ark.

Her favorite subject is menstrual cramps. Followed closely by bowel movements. Actually, excretion of any kind.

Louise, 38, Millville, N.J.

She's forever examining herself for lumps, sores that won't heal, moles with irregular borders. You're sitting next to her, watching a movie, and she's fiddling with herself, feeling her body parts for some kind of dread disease. She'll take your fingers, place them under her arm and say, "There. Feel that lump?"

Marlene, 30, Utica, N.Y.

Do not go into a public bathroom after her. She does not sit down. She pees standing up and splashes all over the seat. After a movie, I run to get in line in front of her. If she's in front of me, I say something like, "Oh look! Someone dropped a five-dollar bill," and scoot ahead.

June, 35, Elgin, Ill.

You can't not laugh when you hear hers. And she's always laughing. It's contagious. It's like being tickled. I simply cannot sit around and be depressed when she's around. Literally—I have to get up and run to make it to the bathroom.

Niki, 45, Seattle, Wash.

She won't leave me alone about my face-lift. She's so jealous that I look spectacular that she constantly makes cracks about my mouth being in my forehead, that if I French kiss, I'll get a lobotomy. She says it's not a dimple, it's my belly button in my chin. I tell her to get her nose shortened; it's got to be too big if it's into my business. But there's no stopping her.

Pamela, 48, Towsend, Md.

She's full-figured, and she doesn't wear underwear. Ever. Depending on what she's wearing and how she's positioned, this can be unsettling.

Cindy, 32, Tucson, Ariz.

77

Nothing's left of Cass that's original. She's done her boobs, lips, nose, eyes, jaw, fanny, tummy, veins. Her hair's a different color every time I see her. I've got old photographs, though. She'd better be nice to me.

Leah, 56, Coral Gables, Fla.

She compares our bodies. She tells me I'm a Modigliani; she's a Reubens. She's furious because I have no thigh bulge.

Greta, 39, Washington, D.C.

She smokes. I won't allow it in my house, so she spends her time out on the porch. In a two-hour visit, she might be inside for all of fifteen minutes.

Juditha, 32, Buffalo Grove, Ill.

Libby defies aging. I don't know how. Good genes? A good plastic surgeon? Baths in the blood of virgins? All I know is, I'm ten months younger than she is and people think I'm her mother.

Carolyn, 53, Doylestown, Pa.

She sucks through her teeth after she eats.

Ellyn, 22, Chatham, N.C.

Marcia has a calorie counter, and she takes it with her to restaurants. Everything you order, she tells you its fat content and calories per serving.

Wendy, 26, Denver, Colo.

I've stopped, but she still smokes. If I complain that her clothes stink of cigarettes, she bathes herself in so much perfume that I can't breathe. Choose your poison.

Charlene, 37, Waukegan, Ill.

She clicks her dentures, poor thing. But, really, I want to climb the walls.

Gwendolyn, 73, Broomall, Pa.

Sharon chews with her mouth open, smacks her lips, talks with her mouth full. She basically does everything at the table that your mother ever told you *not* to do.

Jill, 25, Toledo, Ohio

Our whole lives, we've pigged out together. Now, all of a sudden, at the age of 37, she's keeping kosher. She won't eat in my house anymore. We can only eat out at truly kosher restaurants. I may be cynical, but I suspect this whole thing was cooked up so she could redo her kitchen and get new dishes. I give it another six months, tops.

Sima, 41, Scarsdale, N.Y.

I'm always offering her mints, gum, mouth spray—anything to cover the onions. You can keel over, but that won't stop her from eating them. She says if it bothers me, I should eat them, too. For her birthday, I gave her mouthwash.

Priya, 32, Salem, Mass.

She counts my cigarettes.

Mavis, 33, New York, N.Y.

She snorts when she laughs. And, I mean, loud. Like, maybe, a charging rhino.

Amber, 21, Nashville, Tenn.

nytime there's an unpleasant odor of any kind, she says real loud, "Paula, excuse yourself." She thinks this is a laugh riot.

Paula, 27, Austin, Tex.

e've been friends for several years. For all that time, we've belonged to the same church, volunteered at the hospital, gone to lunch together. If I'm sick, she calls to see if I need anything. She tells me about men she dates; I tell her about my husband and kids. So, imagine my surprise when I went to see her perform in a community theater and I heard people whispering about her, that they knew her when she was still a man.

Jane, 32, Green Bay, Wis.

Lisa's very physical. She tripped my niece and two classmates to get the bouquet at my wedding. She's good to hang onto if you want good seats at a movie or to make your way through a bargain basement. But do not get between her and the buffet table.

Sonia, 28, Albany, N.Y.

CHAPTER 3

PECKING ORDER

"If She Weren't My Best Friend, I'd Kill Her!"

Throughout the animal kingdom, within each flock, gaggle, or herd, there's one female who dominates the others. And human females are no exception. Some women attempt dominance through openly bossy, demanding, or attention-getting behavior; others, through less obvious, indirect actions or subtle manipulations. Margaret complains, "Minutes before we're supposed to meet, like clockwork, Cybil calls and says she's running late. So I'm sitting there, dressed and ready, twiddling my thumbs, feeling foolish. At her beck and call."

Even the most dominant women, though, are not immune to challenge. In fact, some friendships have evolved from and revolve around power struggles. Through put-downs and one-ups, snide comments and silent treatments, women take shots at friends who too flagrantly flaunt the role of Queen Bee or Mother Hen. Laced with hair-frizzing sweetness or sizzling sarcasm, these parlays for power are amazingly well tolerated among close friends. Probably because they are.

I have to call her. She never picks up the phone to call me. It's always been like that. If I test it and don't call for a week, we just don't talk for a week. When I finally call, she acts wounded. Where have I been?

Rebecca, 33, Providence, R.I.

She's always late. If you're meeting her for lunch, you sit at the table waiting for an eternity. She has the lateness thing down cold, so that she arrives just as you're about to give up and leave. And no matter how late *you* arrive, she's still another half hour. At least.

Cindy, 33, Philadelphia, Pa.

Peg is the most competitive person I know. She *has* to win. It doesn't matter what it is. Not just tennis or bridge. I'm talking about Chinese checkers. Ping-Pong. Canasta. Hangman. Whatever the arena, whoever the opponent—even a five-year-old kid, she has to win. I've seen her cheat at Solitaire.

Molly, 42, Champaign, Ill.

Rhonda bets me about how many days until a guy will call me after a first date. About *whether* he'll call. If I'm wrong and she's right, that makes her day. Doesn't matter if the guy's a creep or a babe, or if I'm going to sit home on Saturday night because he didn't call. She's just got to win the bet.

Judy, 22, Winston-Salem, N.C.

Ida complains, to *me*, that nobody really likes her, that she can't count on anyone, that she has no true friends. So what am I? Chopped liver? A hunk of pastrami? I just nod and say, "Poor dear. It must be tough."

Liz, 44, Lansing, Mich.

Whatever happens to her is the best, or the worst, that ever happened to anyone in all of history. She gets the best price on her car, which is the best car ever made. She gets the biggest raises ever given. She goes out with the best-looking guy, has the best, most amazing time. She gets the worst cramps, has the best sex. She makes the biggest, most obvious exaggerations.

Fran, 26, Bismarck, N.D.

She's got call waiting. She gets the calls; I do the waiting. Really, every time I call her, she puts me on hold.

Debbie, 22, Pittsburgh, Pa.

Whatever problem I ever have, Laura always has worse. She has to outdo me. I had a tough pregnancy, but hers was tougher. My baby was colicky; hers was, too, only worse. It goes on and on. Her house needs more repair work. Her allergies are worse. She has more stress. Worse varicose veins. I swear, if I get a cold, she'll get pneumonia. If my husband has an affair, hers'll have a bigger, more passionate one—with a man.

Sara, 28, Santa Fe, N.Mex.

Faith changes our plans at the last minute if something "better" comes up. She tells me she knows I'll understand.

Kendra, 23, Hollywood, Calif.

She's had her heart broken in more pieces than Humpty Dumpty, had more affairs than Mata Hari, and she emotes more than Sarah Bernhardt, in great detail, about each of them. She gets off on being more worldly than I am, and tells me somberly that I was smart to marry my high school boyfriend. That while I'll never experience great passion, I've saved myself so much pain.

Lynne, 33, Santa Fe, N.Mex.

She looked in the mirror and said, "Don't you think you look better at 40 than at 20?—Well, I don't mean *you* personally . . . women, in general." Then she preened some more.

Doris, 42, Bryn Mawr, Pa.

93

No matter what you're talking about, Norma has to know more about it. She's read more, seen more, heard more, traveled more, dated more, suffered more, worked more, shopped more, tasted more. There's nothing, absolutely nothing you can experience that she isn't already an expert on. Except maybe silence.

Lorna, 24, Pittsburgh, Pa.

Jean's an expert on everything. She'll tell you what to do with your garden, your decorating, your makeup, your wardrobe. Your health, your marriage, your kids. Anything. You don't even have to ask her; she'll tell you.

Colleen, 35, Cleveland, Ohio

She tells you the end of movies you haven't seen yet. If you're at the movies *with* her, she leans over and tells you how she *thinks* it will end. Then she spends days saying, "I told you it would end that way. I could have written the script."

Ivy, 34, Des Moines, Iowa

Diane has rules about everything. You have to use proper language, never colloquialisms. No cursing. You have to be prompt and properly attired. Accurate in every statement, tasteful in every topic. The rules are never spoken; they're just implied. But if you don't adhere to them, your friendship's endangered. You're history. Outta heah.

Lynda, 24, Bethesda, Md.

She's so organized. So competent. Christmas cards out on time. Full-time job, gourmet dinner at six, house clean, kids well-dressed, polite, accomplished. Laundry done. Body of a model. I hate her.

Susie, 31, Exton, Pa.

She has to pick the restaurant, but I have to make the reservations. Like I'm her secretary. She picks the movie, the time we go see the movie, the seats we sit in. Not that she's controlling or anything.

Casey, 23, New York, N.Y.

Darcy recommended a hairdresser who gave me a perm so bad I had to have five inches cut off my hair. The cleaning people she told me to hire broke the living room mirror. She advised me to use her accountant, so now I have three years of underpaid taxes and fines to pay. And she *still* tells me what to do. She gives the *worst* advice. And I *take* it.

Eleanor, 56, Richmond, Va.

She doesn't tell you her opinions until it's too late. I get my hair restyled, I hear, "Thank *God* you finally got rid of those bangs!" I wear a new outfit, she says, "I'm so glad you didn't show up in that same old dull grey suit." I get a new coat, she says, "Oh, no—without that old blue rag, how will I recognize you?"

Maura, 41, Minneapolis, Minn.

If you're telling Ilene about something that she thinks is trivial, she emanates a definite disdain. You think she's not listening. Until she interrupts you to correct some small detail. "It was Kramer, not George. And not at the coffee shop. It was at the movie theater." And then she resumes her look of bored disdain.

Beth, 27, Santa Fe, N.Mex.

It's tough to get a compliment out of her. The highest compliment you can get, really, is her silence. She'll come into your house and say, "You should ask Marge who does her cleaning." She'll step into your living room and say, "I know a place to get great prices on window treatments." She'll pipe up, "You must be getting tired of your car." Or, "Need the name of an exterminator?" She sees every spot on your carpet, every weed in your yard. And she lets you know it.

Rosemary, 38, Medford, N.J.

Cheryl volunteers herself to death, and then she complains that she has no time to talk, much less play tennis or meet for coffee. She's so needed, so irreplaceable, so important. You feel like a slug for having any leisure time at all.

Ronnie, 41, Sioux City, Iowa

Vera never gets to the point. She goes on and on, as if she thinks you know what she's talking about, but she never comes out and says it. She refers to her nephew's diagnosis, but doesn't reveal it. She talks about the feud with her in-laws, but doesn't say what it's about. She talks around things, leaves you hanging, salivating, if she can.

Melissa, 40, Selma, Ala.

She tells the truth with a vengeance. She'll be the first—probably the only one—to tell you, "You look *awful!*" or "My goodness, how could you wear *that?*"

Whitney, 26, Cleveland, Ohio

101

Mary never forgets a birthday. She remembers to send cards, flowers, gifts not only to me, but to my kids, my sister, my mother. She makes me feel terribly inadequate, because I never remember to send her kids anything. Hell, I don't even remember my *own* family's birthdays until her cards or gifts arrive.

Caroline, 51, Waukegan, Ill.

Sheila sets you up to flatter her. She won't let up until you tell her how great or smart or beautiful she is. She'll moan, "I look awful." Or, "I'm so clutzy." She won't stop until you say she's graceful or pretty. Or whatever. Then she'll argue with you, so you have to work to build her up.

Helene, 31, Denver, Colo.

102

She takes credit for every idea I ever had, everything I've ever accomplished. It's due to her that I drive what I drive, live where I live, work where I work, eat what I eat, wear what I wear. According to her, the only reason I know anything or do anything right is that she told me so.

Kendra, 22, Athens, Ga.

We travel together, and she just assumes that she gets first pick of beds in the hotel room, berths on the cruise ship, seats on the plane. She takes the inside seat at restaurant booths. If I set up a lounge chair at the beach, she sits on it. If I open a door, she walks through.

Laurie, 33, Raleigh, N.C.

103

When we go somewhere together—plays or movies, parties, whatever—Bev assumes I'll do the driving, that I'll drop her at the door and go park somewhere. It's fine with her that I trudge through snow, rain, darkness, or heat by myself while she takes a seat or gets a drink. Don't ask if she pays half the parking—don't even *think* about the gas.

Roz, 42, Highland Park, Ill.

Her compliments leave bruises. Like she'll say, "You look healthy; you've put on weight." Or, "The extra weight looks good on you—the lines don't show as much."

Leslie, 32, San Jose, Calif.

nnie has to be the giver, not the receiver. She invites us, but won't come to our house—when we invite her, she turns it around so we end up at her house again. It's on her turf, under her roof, or not at all.

Penny, 37, Rosemont, Pa.

etty pulls out her diamond drop when women from her club are around. She flashes her rings. She tells me I'm the only one she can be "real" with. So what does that mean? That I'm no threat? That I'm not on her social plane? Not part of the significant upwardly mobile scene? I mean, she doesn't bother to put on *makeup* for me, much less display her baubles.

Beth, 34, Bethesda, Md.

She makes comments like, "Your new bifocals are wonderful—they make your eyes look much bigger. And the frames hide the bags under your eyes."

Carol, 49, Davenport, Iowa

It's not that she's secretive, but I find stuff out *after* it happens. She tells me she's been seeing someone new after they break up. She drives up in a new car; she never told me about getting it. She doesn't tell me that she's going on vacation until she stops by to drop off her parakeet. If I ask why she doesn't tell me anything, she insists she did. She says, "I *must* have told you. I told *everyone*."

Connie, 30, Tulsa, Okla.

She has a certain, loud laugh that, when you hear it, you know she doesn't mean it, but she wants to attract someone's attention. To have him think she's having fun. That she's fun to be around. A regular riot.

Rena, 27, Medford, N.J.

We're very close. Like sisters. I know everything about her friends, her family, her men. Except I've never met any of them. Shari never includes me at social events. She never calls me at home. Our whole relationship exists in the office. Nine to five.

Danielle, 26, Albany, N.Y.

Phyllis ignores my weight. She's thin, and she eats all the time, whatever she wants—doughnuts, bagels, ice cream. That's bad enough, but she shoves half her candy bar in my face. She orders fries, onion rings for the table and says, "Lighten up. You can't diet *all* the time."

Camiel, 42, St. Louis, Mo.

When we run into people she knows, she never introduces me. I introduce myself or stand there like I'm invisible.

Wynnie, 22, Lake Forest, Ill.

Whenever she meets anyone new, she works the conversation around to tell them how important she is. That she graduated from Yale. That she's a lawyer in a big firm. That she's been to Europe seven times, traveled throughout Southeast Asia, once met Sylvester Stallone on an airplane. Sometimes it's hard for her to work all of this into a conversation, but she manages. She's smart. After all, she went to Yale.

Paige, 34, Washington, D.C.

When she wants to get her way, Inger pouts, whines, and talks like a baby. You know she's manipulating you, and she knows you know, but you'll do anything to get her to stop. So it works.

Marsha, 25, Albuquerque, N.Mex.

We've been friends for twenty years. To this day, I have no idea what her opinions are about politics or religion or abortion or any controversial subject. She never reveals them. But she'll tell you what color to paint your family room, or what to serve for a dinner party, and she'll give a twenty-minute lecture on how you could improve the condition of your skin; forty minutes on how to replant your garden.

Michelle, 36, Evanston, Ill.

Marilyn's a schoolteacher, and she talks to me real slow, as if I'm one of her second-graders. In singsong. When I go out, she tells me to be careful. She tells me not just what time the movie starts, but when and exactly where to meet her, and also how to dress, how much cash to bring, where to park, and not to forget to wear warm gloves. Then she reviews everything, to make sure I've got it.

Sadie, 47, New York, N.Y.

Ivy whispers. You can't hear her unless her lips are in your hair. You have to strain. She makes you work to hear her, so she has your full attention.

Julie, 27, Minneapolis, Minn.

I can't keep food in the house when she's around. She comes in, invades my fridge, helps herself, complains that the roast is too rare, that I'm out of mustard. I hide the good stuff in the back, but she finds it. And she never puts anything away.

Bonnie, 29, Brookline, Mass.

If you press Bonnie for a recipe, she'll dodge. "It's got a little of this, a pinch of that. You know." Or she'll leave out one critical ingredient. If you ask where she bought a certain pair of shoes or a bathing suit, she can't remember. She says she'll try and find the receipt. If you ask where her kids take ballet, she'll say it's somewhere downtown. But don't bother calling; there's a waiting list.

Tracey, 36, Amherst, N.Y.

Mae is smug about her religion. She behaves as if her personal friends are angels and she's in direct contact with the Almighty Himself. Every day she proclaims how blessed she is. As if she's the only one.

Harriet, 66, Darien, Conn.

113

I can't win with Anna. If I say I'm tired, she says I should get up and push myself. If I say I should do more, she tells me to rest. If I say the cake's too rich, she says you have to have *some* calories. If I say I like the cake, she says it's too rich. If I say we better hurry, she says we have time. If I say we have time, she tells me to step on it.

Celia, 27, Corpus Christi, Tex.

I drive everywhere. She directs. She tells me to go faster, slower, take a shortcut through the alley. If she doesn't like my radio station, she changes it. If it starts drizzling, she reaches over and turns on the wipers. If my phone rings, she answers it. It's usually for her.

Audrey, 25, Portland, Ore.

She believes that each person creates their own universe. If you have problems, it's because you've *willed* them into your existence. Everything around you is there by your creation. So, when you're, say, looking for a parking spot, you're supposed to visualize one right where you want it and use your mental energy to create it. If I'm driving and can't find a spot, it means I'm weak, not getting my energy out there. If she's driving and *she* can't find a spot, it's gotta be that I'm sending out negativity that's blocking her energy. It's my fault, not hers.

Imogene, 41, Phoenix, Ariz.

She never comes empty-handed; she brings her own food. A snack. Not for both of us, mind you. Never for two. Just enough for her. One donut. Half a ham sandwich. A chicken leg. Whatever. She never takes any of *my* food, and never offers me a crumb. She'll sit and let me watch her eat. If I say, "That looks good," she nods and says it's delicious. She comes over, munches, finishes her snack, and leaves. I don't get it. Maybe she wants me to admire her food.

Natalie, 31, Ithaca, N.Y.

andy got married at eighteen, had four kids, and went to college and medical school while running a home and being a mom of four preschoolers. But that didn't convince her that she's smart. She's always unsure, takes practice SATs from those books to see how she'd do today. When she tells people her scores, she can't understand that they're not impressed.

Roz, 40, Rochester, N.Y.

t Chinese restaurants, she takes my cookie, reads my fortune. If she likes mine better than hers, she switches. She says, "You took my cookie." I'm not kidding. She thinks she can grab someone else's fortune just by eating their cookie.

Claudia, 30, Medord, N.J.

117

When Faye compliments me, I usually feel insulted. Maybe because of all the hyperbole. She'll say, "That's absolutely the best meal you've ever cooked." Or, "Your hair looks better than it ever did." So, like, were all my other meals mediocre? Did my hair look really awful before?

Lilly, 26, Chevy Chase, Md.

I'm divorced, so she never invites me to couples' stuff, but she tells me what a blast everyone had, and then she gets embarrassed, explains that she wishes I could have been there, but she knows how uncomfortable I'd have felt, being there alone. Well, I know how uncomfortable *she'd* have felt.

Britanny, 30, Topeka, Kans.

118

She's chairman of this, president of that. And then, she has too much to do and no time to do it, so she assigns me jobs. "Helene—I need two dozen cookies by tomorrow for the bake sale." "Helene—I need you to sort and deliver 195 sweatshirt and T-shirt orders." "Helene—tonight can you build fourteen solar system mobiles for Science Week?" I'd have a much less hectic life if she didn't take on so much responsibility.

Helene, 33, Radnor, Pa.

If I'm driving, I go to her door and ring the bell. If she's driving, she sits in the car and honks the horn.

Donna, 28, Springfield, Ill.

119

PERSONALITY

"If She Weren't My Best Friend, I'd Kill Her!"

Our personalities are affected by a multitude of factors—hormones, health, weather, work, love, luck, phases of the Moon, positions of the planets, exposure to sunlight, heavy traffic, bad hair. Anything and everything can bring out the best or worst in us. Our moods fluctuate. Our temperaments change. So that finding compatible companionship can be a challenge: What pleases us about a friend one day may drive us mad about them the next. And vice versa.

Over the course of time, most friends accept each other's moods, understanding the ebbs and flows, waiting out the tough times, trying to keep in sync. For friendship's sake, many of us tolerate talking when we prefer silence, cheeriness when we feel glum. Some of us alter our behavior to conform to our friends' moods du jour.

But there are limits. Even in the most devoted friendships, there are times when one pal's nature aggravates the other. "Sometimes," Marilyn swears, "Izzy gets under my skin so bad that I itch. I get hives hearing her voice."

Depending upon our moods and theirs, those we know and love best may appeal to us least. How we react—and what qualities we react to—tells us a lot about our friends and friendships. And even more about ourselves.

She cries all the time. About anything. Birthdays. Sunsets. How nice a time we're having. She's always holding soggy tissues, wiping her tears. Perpetually mourning the continuous demise of the present.

Betty, 32, Houston, Tex.

She calls me "Dahling." She calls *everybody* "Dahling." And everything's "mahvelous." I think she thinks it makes her sound glamorous. Kind of a Zsa Zsa thing.

Dodie, 63, Buffalo, N.Y.

Lois is cheerful, no matter what. She always finds a bright spot. If you've smashed your car, she'll say, "At least no one was hurt." If someone *was* hurt, she'd say, "At least no one was killed." If someone *was* killed, she'd say, "At least it wasn't you." If it *was* you, she'd probably find something good about that, too. Like, "At least you didn't suffer."

Angela, 39, Laguna Beach, Calif.

Being happy depresses her; she thinks it's dangerous. If things are up, they can only go down. Anything fun will eventually be over, so why enjoy it? Why set yourself up for a loss? The only emotion she trusts is melancholy. If she thinks *I'm* riding too high, she does her best to bring me down—for my own good, of course.

Debbie, 41, Smyrna, Ga.

The girl has more locks on her doors than she has fingers. If you need to go to the bathroom while she's unlocking, sorting through her keys, figuring out which one goes where, there could be a problem.

Kalila, 49, Albany, N.Y.

Rose cannot talk about herself. She never gives herself credit for anything, not an idea or an action. You'd never know that she has a Ph.D. in history or that she was in the Peace Corps. She's so shy that when other people are around, I have to talk for her.

Marsha, 32, Willow Grove, Pa.

If I compliment something, she'll give it to me. If I tell her I liked her beef stew, she makes me take home the leftovers. If I say I like her scarf, I have to wear it home. She gave me a ring with a diamond chip in it, insisted I take it. I've thought of complimenting her car . . .

Bea, 34, San Diego, Calif.

Monica refuses to dwell on disturbing thoughts. If she has a problem—with money, work, romance, health—or whatever, she says, "Let's just not think about it," and ignores it. She seems to think that if you ignore a problem long enough it'll resolve itself or go away. So far, this has worked for her. She glides through life and somehow, just when she's flat broke, the rent appears. Just when she's giving up on men, she meets a new guy. Just when she thinks she's dying, she gets over the flu. Why worry?

Patsy, 34, Boston, Mass.

She's very open. She'll tell you everything about herself. Her family. Me. My family. Everything.

Barbara, 38, Taos, N.Mex.

126

Kate is completely irreverent, and she makes me laugh at inappropriate times. Like in the middle of a wedding. On the way there, she said, "You know, it would be really terrible if someone burst out laughing right while they're taking their vows." That was it. I couldn't help it. Oh, and at her uncle's funeral, she whispered it was good he was already dead because, otherwise, the price of the coffin would kill him. And if not that, then the sight of Aunt Fritzie's hat. I laughed. She gets me in trouble. She has since high school.

Marsha, 26, Greenville, S.C.

She analyzes everything. Finds meaning in anything. In how somebody looks at her, how firmly he shook her hand. How long they paused before asking, "How are you?" She traces the deep motives and meaning of every teensy action or reaction. Why did you stop at the cleaners before coming to get her? Or why did you call your sister before you called her? Nothing's too small for her to obsess on.

Gina, 42, Tulsa, Okla.

You can't curse around her. She's too good a soul. Pure at heart. Her skin glows, and when you're around her, you think about going to church again.

Dodie, 31, Independence, Oreg.

She never comes over empty-handed. She brings me wine, chocolates, flowers. So when I go to her house, I never go empty-handed. I bring her wine. Chocolates. Flowers. I wish we could just call it even.

Edie, 26, Portland, Maine

She claims to be psychic. Every time something happens—anything—from a bad haircut to a terrorist attack—she says, "Oh, I *knew* it! I had a feeling that would happen." When I call her, she says, "I *knew* it was you." She calls to tell me to be careful; she's had a premonition about me. Then, if nothing happens, obviously, it's because she warned me. If something happens—no matter what it was—she was right. She *knew* it.

Margie, 38, Wilmington, Del.

Abby mumbles to herself all the time. Even if I'm in the room with her. I ask, "What did you say?" She says, "Nothing—I wasn't talking to you."

Jodie, 38, Santa Fe, N.Mex.

She's logical and practical. This is good because she gives you a good listen and has a bottom-line, no-nonsense approach to your choices, options, courses of action. But you can't whine to her. She has no appreciation for the subtle variations of suffering, the incremental levels of misery. When I want to wallow, I call someone else.

Carol, 34, Portland, Oreg.

Her house has no clutter and no dust. If you start to put a drink down, she slides a coaster under it. The second you finish drinking, the glass is rinsed, dried, and put away.

Gladys, 32, Mobile, Ala.

131

I'm not saying she's superstitious, but Lorraine backs up and drives around the block if she sees a black cat crossing the street. She throws salt over her shoulder, carries a purseful of good-luck coins, and wears a bracelet of lucky charms. She also won't eat the last piece of anything because she doesn't want to be an old maid.

Diane, 28, Providence, R.I.

She calls and says, "So, what do you know?" This irritates me. I want to irritate her back, so I answer, "Nothing. What do *you* know?" She gets irritated and replies, "Not a single thing." This routine is repeated every morning, word for word.

Yasmine, 34, Boston, Mass.

She's seen a shrink for, like, twenty years. How can you talk about yourself for twenty years? Wouldn't you get bored? Wouldn't you get sick of hashing the same stuff over and over? What do you do when you run out of things to say about yourself? Do you move on to other subjects? Like, maybe, your friends? Their lives? Their problems? In twenty years, she should have solved *all* our problems—hers, mine, her parents', her husband's, everyone's on the street.

Lorraine, 42, Darien, Conn.

She's not a snob to *me*, but if she doesn't know you, she figures she doesn't need to. And doesn't bother.

Helene, 33, Cambridge, Mass.

133

She mocks me if I complain about anything. "You *poor* dear," she says sarcastically. "That is *so* sad." Or else she cuts me off, "Don't start." Or, "Oh, please." And she changes the subject as if I hadn't said anything.

Tomika, 28, Washington, D.C.

Her therapist's like Rasputin. She won't do anything unless he approves. She asks him before she'll go out with a new guy. She won't move to a new place, take a vacation, start a diet, join a book club, ask for a raise without his okay. She'll never quit therapy—she'd need his permission.

Chloe, 31, Chevy Chase, Md.

When she's depressed, Myra cleans. She throws out everything, her kids' toys, her husband's gadgets. She vacuums, she scrubs. If you walk in the door and trip over laundry, you know she's fine. But if there's not a speck of dust in her house, you know she's got trouble.

Laura, 29, Little Rock, Ark.

She tells me her dreams. No, not what she hopes for. What she *dreams*. She calls at eight in the morning and says, "So, my mother was at the *computer*—of all things—and my cousin Norma walked in carrying a peach pie but I couldn't find a fork, so I went through about eight different hallways to get my shoes, but someone was following me, a woman, I think, but then I couldn't find my mother *or* the computer. . . ." She spares me no details. But it's not enough that I have to listen to the whole involved story. She wants me to analyze it.

Martha, 31, Lexington, Ky.

She's dresses great, looks fabulous. But if you step into her apartment, you trip over things. Climb over shoes, cereal boxes, and dead plants to get to the furniture. When I asked her why she doesn't put her laundry away, she sighed that she'd only have to take it out again. There was no place to sit, so I picked up a pile of stuff and the cordless phone fell out. She was delighted, and exclaimed, "Great! I've been *looking* for that for days."

Debra, 24, Washington, D.C.

Libby's a terrible cook. Terrible. She invited me to dinner and served a hamburger and ketchup omelette.

Mona, 27, Seattle, Wash.

137

ou don't want to ride in her car. You'll sit in jelly stains and dog hair. There's a training potty in the backseat and toilet paper in the back so she won't have to stop to take her kids to the bathroom. She has a change of clothes for the little one, spare shoes, odd toys, books, snacks. But there's always something to eat, if you're hungry.

Nina, 22, Albany, N.Y.

Susan talks in food. Women are tomatoes. Her husband's a peach, but he's got bagels around his middle. Her mother-in-law's a prune. Her daughter's a cookie, tamale, or cupcake, but her daughter's boyfriend treats her like chopped liver. He's a hunk of spoiled beef, a piece of bad meat. Something her daughter should slice, dice, chew up, and spit out.

Janice, 27, Toms River, N.J.

Joyce hibernates in the winter. You don't see her or hear from her. She resurfaces in March or April. She says it's a light deprivation thing. She doesn't go anywhere, doesn't even return calls in December.

Millie, 51, Twin Falls, Idaho

Miranda's always networking. "You never know who you'll meet, or how they might help you out one day." Anywhere we go, she chats with strangers, tells her life story, gives out her name, shakes hands. You'd think she was running for office.

Brooke, 32, Flint, Mich.

Vicki follows the crowd. She strives to be "normal." Her opinions are based on what she thinks most other people think. She'd never take a stand, unless everyone around her did first. The woman won't order her lunch without knowing what everyone else at the table is going to have, and she selects from among their choices.

Denise, 30, Richmond, Va.

Freda doesn't censor herself. Not in public, not around families. She uses language that isn't acceptable, but you can't tell her. Or she'll use it on you.

Marilyn, 31, Louisville, Ky.

laudia speaks Corporatese. If I'm hassled, she tells me, "Reorganize, prioritize, and redefine your goals." If I mention that my kids are driving me nuts, she says, "You need to restructure your organizational patterns before they impact upon your overall parenting effectiveness." And she'll rattle that kind of thing off without cracking a smile.

Doreen, 32, Providence, R.I.

hen they get depressed, some people get drunk. Some people shop. Some people go party. When Pam's depressed, which is often, she eats chocolate. And she never does it alone. Have I mentioned that *she* never puts on a pound?

142

Tania, 24, Southfield, Mich.

Michelle cannot cut to the chase. She needs to tell you every detail. If she were telling you about a murder, she'd tell you the clothes they wore, the food they ate, the weather that night, how traffic was on the highway, who she coincidentally knew who'd once lived on the same street as the cousin of the victim, before she'd get around to telling you who killed whom.

Brenda, 23, Urbana, Ill.

She keeps lists not just of chores for the day, but of films to see, restaurants to go to, recipes to try out, people to invite, books to read. She checks them off when she's done. She keeps lists for her kids, too. Of things they should experience. Places they should travel. Crafts they should learn. Sports they should master. Books they should read and vacations they should take. Courses the kids should take in college.

Erika, 30, Glencoe, Ill.

She knows every rumor there is. Well, I mean, she *ought* to. After all, she started most of them.

Jan, 29, Shaker Heights, Ohio

Cheryl chats with everyone she makes eye contact
with. That means maître d's, waitresses, salespeople,
garage attendants, receptionists. When you go
anywhere with her, you stand around, waiting for
her to finish talking with strangers so you can have
a conversation.

Amy, 23, Tucson, Ariz.

No matter how good her life is, Eva finds
something to complain about. She thinks it's bad luck
to be content—people resent you and the Evil Eye will
curse you if you let on that you're happy. But that
shouldn't really bother her; it would give her plenty to
complain about.

Tillie, 29, Denver, Colo.

145

She blurts out whatever's on her mind, has no censor mechanism. In the middle of a crowd, in the middle of a conversation, she'll announce, "Oh, no! I just got my period!" Or, "Damn. I forgot to shave my legs *again!*"

Lisa, 22, Hollingdale, N.J.

The woman's a genius at her job, but she knows nothing, not a single thing else. She has no common sense. Instead of replacing the batteries, she buys a new flashlight. If she pops a button, she buys a new coat. If she had to eat her own cooking, she'd starve. It's a good thing she can afford help; she really needs it.

Lonnie, 35, Brentwood, Calif.

She's out to save the whales, protect the dolphins. You can't buy that brand of tuna, or teak or mahogany. She boycotts fur. Protests animal testing. You can't wear makeup around her.

Marissa, 38, Portland, Oreg.

Everything Trudy tells me begins with, "Swear you won't tell anybody I told you this?" Or, "This is supposed to be a secret, so don't tell anyone else, okay?" I love her, but I don't dare tell her anything I don't want broadcast all over the neighborhood. On the other hand, when I want something broadcast, I just tell her it's a secret and let her do her thing.

Evelyn, 31, Cincinnati, Ohio

Sylvia told a PTA member that her bundt cake wasn't underbaked—she should just relabel it "pudding." At brunch, her niece was breast-feeding at the table. Sylvia passed her a coffee cup, asked for a dollop of cream. She's the most sarcastic person I know.

Lila, 43, Lexington, Ky.

rowing up, I was the good one; Christie was always in trouble, plunging into whatever she felt like. Her boyfriend got a convertible, so they kidnapped me from my job and took me to Lake Geneva. I went to grad school in Colorado; one day she and some guy dropped by for a visit. She lived in Chicago. I wasn't home, so she left me a note and headed for Las Vegas. She eloped with a guy she met on an airplane, married him that same day. And marriage hasn't changed her. A few weeks ago we were supposed to have lunch; that morning I got a telegram breaking our date. Seems it was Carnival in Rio.

Kathy, 24, Wilmette, Ill.

She's always a party. She's always got to have fun. You can't just relax and let your mind float. In the dentist's waiting room, she's doing crossword puzzles with you. Waiting for the plane to take off, she makes you play "Twenty Questions" or "Four Fourths of a Ghost." She never just sits. And she won't let you, either.

Jodie, 21, Minneapolis, Minn.

Fran never hurries. I don't think she *can* hurry. She moves at a consistent, slow, and steady pace. Her plane can be about to take off, but she'll stroll to the gate. A truck can be barreling toward her, and she'll raise an eyebrow at the driver and step grudgingly out of the way.

Clarissa, 52, Sarasota, Fla.

Shari never thinks ahead. She plunges in. And somehow, it's my job to intervene. I'm the one who talked her out of quitting her job and moving to New Zealand. I even got back her letter of resignation before her boss got it. I'm the one who stopped her from getting her old boyfriend's name tattooed on her butt. I talked her out of piercing her tongue. I wear the soles off my shoes, putting on the brakes for her.

Veronica, 20, Norwich, Conn.

She reads romance novels and cries. Sobs. Out loud, goes through boxes of tissues.

Margaret, 38, Hattiesburg, Miss.

151

Forget feminism. Ava does the old blonde and dumb act. She blinks, "How does this work?" And guys cluster around her, explaining computer programs, fixing her car engine, reloading the copier. She strokes them. "You're so smart! What would I have done without your help?" I've seen grown men trample each other to do whatever she needs. It's pitiful. When I ask guys for help, they yawn, "Read the instruction manual."

Darlene, 30, Syracuse, N.Y.

152

Liz never drops a subject. She goes over and over and over it again and again. "But are you *positive* I said the right thing?" "Are you *sure* I shouldn't have bought the pink one?" Revisits every interaction, each decision.

Elissa, 28, Tallahassee, Fla.

er house is always apart. She upholsters furniture to match the wallpaper, then decides she hates the wallpaper. She's always redoing something. And something's always being done in the kitchen—first, it was the counters, then the floor. Now, it's an island with a grill. They've had to eat out for years.

Celia, 34, Columbus, Ohio

he wants me to have more friends and be more open to people, so she pushes me into conversations, tells people my personal business. She'll say, "Lucille, meet Jan. Jan takes Prozac, too." Or "Meet Gina. You think your divorce was ugly—wait till you hear about *hers*."

154

Lucille, 38, Tallahassee, Fla.

Anita never finishes anything. She's all gung ho, and then she drops out, loses interest. Her apartment's a graveyard for unfinished projects. Half-knitted afghans, half-built birdhouses, half-painted watercolors, half-completed poems. She got me to take a karate class. She dropped out and there I was. Now, she's decided to breed terriers. We'll see.

Kaitlyn, 37, Rockland, Maine

She gets bummed out for weeks about characters in soaps. She'll wail, "Oh, no—Tracey lost the baby!" Or "Stephen's cheating on Melanie—and she's dying of a brain tumor!" I don't know what to say to her. She is not amused if I say, "Ruthie—it's just a story."

Miranda, 25, Knoxville, Tenn.

155

oni's completely disorganized. She stops halfway from one place to another to do something completely unrelated. She actually stopped to get her dog shampooed on the way to a picnic. She got to the picnic late, and of course the dog ran into the creek to play in the mud. She's always late, changing plans without warning. She starts getting dressed after her company's arrived. She'll remember to walk the dog in the middle of a dinner party. She'll set out for the supermarket and end up downtown at a museum. The only predictable thing about her is that she's unpredictable. She ricochets like a Ping-Pong ball gone mad.

Samanatha, 31, Chevy Chase, Md.

She never remembers anything. She walks through parking garages, floor by floor, because she can't remember what level she left her car on. She pays for a pair of panty hose with a twenty and forgets to wait for her change, so the saleslady runs after her, shouting for her to come back. She goes back for the change and leaves without her package. This happens all the time.

Sadie, 30, Chicago, Ill.

Latisha sings along with the radio. If there's no radio, she sings anyhow. She says she can't help it; music's in her soul. If it were only in her voice!

Christina, 22, Atlanta, Ga.

157

If the subject isn't about Joan or directly related to her, she stays out of the conversation and waits until she can turn it her way. Then she pounces, grabs the floor, and will not release it. She can promote herself all night long.

Stephanie, 27, Chicago, Ill.

There are days she's all in a dither and spins around like a windup toy gone mad. Like the day her car got stolen. We were halfway downtown when she remembered that she left a pot of eggs on the stove. She backed up into traffic, hit a light post and made a U-turn. When we got home, she found that she'd actually turned the pot off. But, by then, she was so frazzled that she locked the keys in the car and we were stuck in the street, trying to break into it. So she asked some teenage boys to help her. They were glad to. They got into the car, picked up the keys, and drove away, waving to us.

Caitlyn, 30, San Jose, Calif.

159

Do not drive anywhere new with Lindsey, unless you have a map. Even if you're in her own neighborhood. She's not stupid; she's just lost all the time. She has no sense of direction. North, east, west—they're all the same to her. I've explained that, during the day, you can tell which way north is because the Sun rises east and sets west. She said, "Well, except if you're facing the other direction."

Paige, 29, St. Petersburg, Fla.

No matter where I sit in church, I can hear her sing. She hits high notes the composer didn't intend. I mean, I'm pretty sure *no* one's ever heard them before.

Kimberly, 44, Des Moines, Iowa

She's always her good old same old self. She never changes. She wants to go the same place for lunch, and she orders the same tuna on toast. Won't even try a BLT. She has the same complaints about work, the same gripes about her husband. She's never really up or down, always in the same basic mood. We have the same conversations over and over again. Being with her is like visiting the past. A bit dull, but stable and reassuring.

Karen, 39, Ames, Iowa

Kendra's the strongest woman I know. She was suddenly widowed at thirty-two, but she didn't mope, said she'd been lucky to have had the few years they'd had. She's funny, sparkly, open, honest, earthy, caring. I keep looking for flaws in her, but after twelve years, I still can't find any. Except that, by comparison, she makes me feel like a whining, ungrateful, emotional wimp.

Jade, 33, Detroit, Mich.

Phyllis has no sense of humor whatever. If you tell a joke, she looks at you blankly and waits for the laughing to stop. Then she picks up the conversation where it left off.

Patsy, 31, St. Cloud, Minn.

Jill has no idea how powerful she is. People are drawn to her, listen to her, respect her. Want to please her. I've studied her for years, practiced her smile, imitated her listening and nodding techniques. Her facial expressions. Her posture. None of it works for me. It must be her round face, how nonthreatening it is. Or her cute tiny little button nose. Or her adorable big blue eyes. Something . . .

Shawna, 27, Boston, Mass.

When she talks, she uses her hands. If she's excited, you can't stand too close or you'll get whapped.

Lynne, 28, Poughkeepsie, N.Y.

163

Pat has the most outrageous ideas. And she shares them with everybody. Like that everyone should be given one GET OUT OF JAIL FREE card. One free crime, even murder; jail should be only for repeat offenders. She thinks that elections should be eliminated—government should be picked like a jury, by lottery; if your name comes up, you're president. You serve. She has dozens of these. Maybe I'm with her too much; some of them are actually beginning to make sense.

Maggie, 37, Pittsburgh, Pa.

Florence is diplomatic about herself, blunt about you.

Gloria, 50, Manchester, N.H.

Mimi sees the worst side of things and always shares her perspective with you. If you get a new car, she comments about how it will devalue in two years. If you go on vacation, she remarks that coming back will suck. If you go out with a new guy, she says, what's going to be wrong with this one?

Ellen, 28, Raleigh, N.C.

165

anie laughs at me. I swear, I don't know why. And she won't tell me. All of a sudden, she just laughs out loud and says, "I love you. You're great." Then she laughs some more.

Ann, 22, Bloomington, Ind.

oannie is the biggest liar I've ever met. To her, it's a challenge to see how big a whopper she can get away with. It's like her sport. She'll say anything with a completely straight look—like she won a gold medal in the '72 Olympics. Or she's Clark Gable's illegitimate child. But I can always tell when she's lying because she swears on her Great Grandma Winifred's grave. That's the dead giveaway.

June, 42, Rapid City, N.D.

I swear, I'm her only friend. She's miserable, selfish, and often quite nasty. She makes no bones about it, either. She declares, "I have no time for women. They're of no use to me." Nobody likes her. When she got married, I thought I should throw a bridal shower for her. But, truly, there was no one to invite. Even her own cousins wouldn't come. All she's got is me. Even *I* don't like her, but *somebody's* got to be her friend.

Dana, 26, St. Paul, Minn.

167

GUYS

Princes or frogs, babes or bums, men fascinate women. What men like or don't, who they'll go out with or won't, the games they play, the lines they say, what they fight about, what they're uptight about, how they dress, how they kiss—when it comes to men, whatever it is, women talk about it.

But talk isn't all we do. After Tom or Dick depart, we keep each other well occupied, at least until Harry comes around.

"Whenever I'm on my own and Jan has no man," says Donna, "I'm her partner for dinner, vacations, movies, concerts—whatever. We're so compatible that, when I meet a new guy, I ask myself, 'Would I rather hang with him or Jan?' Usually, he's out."

Women talk about love and romance, in the process turning battle scars into badges, experience into expertise, loss into lore. When a woman gets dumped, her friends pump her up. If her heart breaks, her friends glue the pieces. If her dude's a dud, they give her the gumption to bump him. And, if she finally finds true love, her friends take a step back. But only one.

Friends may move over to make room for a guy, but they stay within earshot, waiting to hear all about him.

She interrogates me about my dates. Has he stayed over yet? Has he introduced you to his parents? Where does he work? Be sure about safe sex. She acts just like my mother.

Abbey, 26, New York, N.Y.

When Gail dates someone, she addresses them, introduces them, and refers to them by their formal Christian names. Bob was surprised that he was suddenly Robert. Larry, Ned, and Hank became Lawrence, Theodore, Henry. Now she's seeing Paul. I suspect this frustrates her.

Marla, 23, Richmond, Va.

She comes to my house, plops on my sofa and calls her boyfriend. They talk for hours. Literally. Once, they were on my phone from 7:30 to after 10 P.M. When calls come in on call waiting, she takes messages and tells them I'll call back.

Jennifer, 25, Rochester, N.Y.

She's very proud of her condom collection. It's on display on the table in her living room.

Autumn, 26, Phoenix, Ariz.

When we were in high school, we invented these imaginary guys. Lance B. Strong was her dream man. My dream guy was Royce P. Ferguson. We went together to get birth control pills from a clinic, and we registered as Mrs. Strong and Mrs. Ferguson. I still make dinner reservations under that name. And when she's out, I often leave messages that "Mrs. Ferguson called."

Jane, 30, Knoxville, Tenn.

Before my first date, Yvonne taught me how to kiss. She gave me instructions, like how to tilt my head and part my lips, and then she tested me, scolded me for getting it wrong. I can still hear her. "No, not like that—you're too puckered up. Keep them soft!"

Naomi, 29, Kansas City, Mo.

Teresa likes to play matchmaker. She fixes me up now and then and she thinks that gives her the right to know everything that happened on the dates. If a relationship develops, she wants to know everything that happens in the relationship. And I mean everything. Like whether he wears boxers.

Lois, 31, Denver, Colo.

173

She never looks at a guy until I go out with him. Then she suddenly falls in love with him. This has been true since junior high. Once, this boy Dave and I went to a party and by midnight, they were going steady. Over the years I've learned to manage, though. The only reason she's dating Scott now is that I pretended to be mad about him. That way she won't notice how fond I am of Carl.

Danielle, 22, St. Petersburg, Fla.

She doesn't like anyone I date. Ever. Never has. Never will. If I went out with him, she'd find something wrong with Prince Charming.

Cynthia, 25, San Jose, Calif.

She's a lab technician. She's always talking about veins. She doesn't notice if a guy has blue or brown eyes, or if he's got hair. All she notices is how easy it would be to draw his blood.

Latreese, 23, Memphis, Tenn.

MaryEllen's desperate to marry me off. She fixes me up with people I wouldn't spit at. Guys I wouldn't let tie my shoes. She tells me I'm too picky, that I'll be alone all my life. She scolds me for not being attracted to zombies, says, "I don't know why I bother. You won't like any man who's nice to you."

Gloria, 40, Cincinnati, Ohio

I don't like her to meet the guys I date because she always finds fault with them and then I can't look at them the same way again. Greg had pasty skin and Dave had big ears. Ted was kind of swishy. Lou talked like a thug. Not that any of them was fond of her, either.

Lynda, 22, Houston, Tex.

Stacey has me call her boyfriend to make sure he's home working like he says he is. She has me disguise my voice and ask for a bogus name, pretend to be a wrong number. Or pretend I'm selling something. Once he asked a dozen questions about my carpet cleaning special and set up an appointment for an estimate.

Reggie, 27, Washington, D.C.

I've been her friend through two marriages. Now she's on the third, but I'm not to mention the others. It's like those men, those times, and anything we ever did when they were with us don't exist.

Maria, 38, Lexington, Ky.

177

It's not only that she runs personal ads for me. It's that she *answers* them for me, too. And arranges actual dates.

Samantha, 30, Detroit, Mich.

Myra expects me to be close to whoever she's going with. So I become friends with the guy. Then, when she dumps him, I'm supposed to dump him, too. She didn't speak to me for weeks when she found out I exchange Christmas cards with one of her exes. She'd *kill* me if she found out I still play squash with Jeff.

Julia, 34, Bethesda, Md.

arb and I share an apartment. We did our laundry together, ate meals together, went to movies together, shopped together, went on vacations together. Until I met Hank. As I was going to dinner with him one night, she whined, "But I made your favorite *pasta*." She didn't talk to me for three days and sulked around the apartment like a wounded cat.

Inga, 25, Chattanooga, Tenn.

he has no idea how she affects men. No idea how pretty she is. None. She doesn't notice how men crane their necks to watch her walk by, or how cars swerve to avoid drivers watching her instead of the road.

Stephanie, 23, Chicago, Ill.

179

I've been her maid of honor twice. I'm there for her, as many times as she wants me to be. But next time, no wedding shower. And *she* buys the dress.

Lorraine, 37, Waukegan, Ill.

She sees too much goodness in men. So she goes out with complete jackasses. One of her exes broke up with her on her birthday. Not only that, he took her wallet with him, her credit cards and fifty-five dollars cash. She said he only did it because he was humiliated and embarrassed that he had no money of his own to buy her a gift. She forgave him.

Georgia, 36, New Orleans, La.

When we were in high school, I thought it would be funny to send her a valentine from a secret admirer. I've been doing it ever since. She can't figure out who it is. She moves to a new address, but it still comes. She gets married, but it still comes. She has no clue, but she's sure he's married to one of her friends and that's why he can't come forth. If she knew the truth, she'd kill me.

Summer, 26, Seattle, Wash.

Hallie can drink any man under the table. And does. In fact, that's where I met her, under a table. We were at a fraternity party; I stepped on her.

Meg, 22, Ithaca, N.Y.

181

She always picks men who dump on her. It takes me weeks to build her up, make her see that the trouble is him, not her. Then she drops him, feels better, goes out and finds another one, and we start all over again.

Judy, 27, San Diego, Calif.

Libby changes our plans at the last minute whenever something "vitally important" comes up. "Vitally important" means there's a man involved. Or the possibility of meeting a man. She doesn't apologize for this, either. She thinks it's normal and says she knows I'll understand, that I'd do the same to her if I were single.

Sonia, 33, Raleigh, N.C.

She does impressions of her husband, as if he's the dumbest, most inarticulate creature since man stood on two legs. When he's around, she purrs at him like a kitten, bats her eyes, and babies him. It's like he's her pet Neanderthal.

Nina, 28, Taos, N.Mex.

She calls me three or four times a day, except when she's involved with someone. Then I don't hear from her until they break up.

Sally, 30, Columbus, Ohio

Whenever one of us has a date with someone new, she insists we call each other when we get home. Supposedly, this is a safety precaution, to make sure we got home safe and unharmed. But if I don't call her by the time she thinks I *should*, she calls me, so there I am, lip to lip, and the phone rings. If I don't answer, she keeps calling and calling until I do.

Hannah, 26, New York, N.Y.

She's actually jealous of my divorce. Whenever I mention my ex, or about how bummed out I am, she tells me, "Stop feeling sorry for yourself. At least you've been *married*." To her, divorce isn't a trauma; it's a status symbol. Like a Jaguar.

Terri, 32, Charlotte, N.C.

In a glance, Stacey'll know the price of a man's watch, briefcase, shoes, the kind of car he drives. She'll know if his socks are unmatched, inside out, or losing their elastic. She'll tell you the cut and fabric of his suit. The size of his wallet. If you ask her what he looks like, she's clueless. A guy can drop dead if he's not wearing the right shoes.

Amanda, 22, Washington, D.C.

185

She uses code to talk about men. SA is sex appeal. BC is body contact. ZC is zero chemistry; MC major chemistry. GB great bod. GK great kisser. SF suck face. Or flesh, I'm not sure. Anyway, she'll rattle on, like, "He's got such SA and a GB, I'm talking MC. I'd love some BC, to SF. I bet he's a GK." It takes me a while to decode it.

Sally, 27, Orlando, Fla.

If I bump into her when she's out with a man, she pretends she doesn't know me. If I greet her, she doesn't introduce me. If I introduce myself, she glares, hurries away, doesn't talk to me for days.

June, 29, St. Louis, Mo.

She makes me go on her blind dates with her. I'm supposed to "run into" her, just casually happen to be wherever they are. If she introduces me as Miranda Hopkins, I'm *not* supposed to leave. I'm supposed to stick around because she doesn't like the guy. If she introduces me by my real name, that means I can move along and leave them alone. I've spent entire evenings with her and poor guys who're wondering how to get rid of Miranda Hopkins.

Denise, 25, Denver, Colo.

She complains how her husband splashes the toilet rim when he takes a leak. No matter how badly I have to go, I never use their bathroom.

Margo, 27, Madison, Wis.

On Friday nights, she drags me out to singles' clubs, bars. She thinks this is fun. I sit there, fending off drunks, watching her dance with desperate, horny men trying to pick her up or at least get her phone number. She tells me she won't go without me, that I have to get out, loosen up, have fun. I think she just wants a sober ride home.

Madelaine, 32, Darby, Pa.

She's dating a married man. When I confront her about it, tell her it's self-destructive, she tells me I'm nuts. She says she gets all the romance and perks and none of the laundry. I can't listen to it. I tell her I have to go iron my husband's boxers.

Vanessa, 31, Boston, Mass.

can't stand her husband. She always wants to go out as couples, and I'm always putting her off. He's so damned *boring*, dominates conversations, tells the same stories over and over. It's like watching reruns of sitcoms.

Georgia, 30, Stamford, Conn.

She's got two kids in diapers and lives vicariously through my dates. She calls first thing the morning after to find out where we went, what we ate or drank, what he wore, what I wore, what he said, how he kissed, whether he stayed over, how he's hung, how many times we did it. If he's still there, she wants to know if we're about to do it again.

Felicia, 25, Denver, Colo.

She has extramarital affairs. She confides in me about them, in detail, and I don't mean the type of wine they drank. I mean, I know where these guys have scars and moles, and I can describe their best features, best moves.

Allegra, 35, Naples, Fla.

Sharon wouldn't date Prince Charming if he was down on his luck. No men without money. Or, I should say, the *potential* for money. She goes places where she'll meet "the right people." An exclusive health club. Volunteering for conservative political candidates. When I tell her that her values are off, she tells me not to worry; she'll be kind to me when she's rich.

Lucy, 22, Chicago, Ill.

She shares too much with me about her husband. And then, I'm stuck with the knowledge. I know that he sweats in bed and it drips on her when they have sex. I really don't want to know this.

Rita, 31, Battle Creek, Mich.

191

We got engaged at about the same time. She asked if we could try on each other's rings. When she put mine on, she said, "This makes my knuckles look so big. It gets lost on my hand." When I tried on hers and said it was beautiful, she said, "*That* ring would make any hand look good."

Judy, 26, Brookline, Mass.

Right in front of her husband, she tells me, "Now that I'm pregnant, the shop's closed down. He's not coming near me any more. I have no desire." I used to pick on her husband. But no more. Now, I feel sorry for him. Poor guy. I try to be kind to him.

Renee, 26, Palo Alto, Calif.

She claims that she was a virgin when she got married. Yeah. And I *still* am.

Melissa, 27, New York, N.Y.

Gena married my old boyfriend and that's fine with me; I think they're both great. Except she thinks I still have a thing for him, which I don't. So it's hard for me to be with them because I have to pretend I don't know him as well as I do. I sometimes accidentally refer to the past or mention a private event—like a movie we saw together. She gets insecure and nuts and he smiles. Seeing her jealous seems to give him a kick.

Lanie, 27, Philadelphia, Pa.

She's having work done on her house. She e-mails me at work to describe the painter's butt, pecs, and shoulders. She tells me how steamed she is, writes me her fantasies. My secretary howls, passes the mail around the office.

Lynne, 36, Wilmington, Del.

She had four kids, each a year apart, says she gets pregnant every time they have sex. And I don't think she's joking.

Virginia, 35, Pearl, Miss.

Everything is related to penises. That's all she talks about. Penis symbols. Penis envy. Penis size. She explains not only individual behavior, but the entire rise and fall of civilizations, in terms of penis size. If Hitler had been better endowed, she's convinced he wouldn't have wrought so much destruction on others. If her husband had a smaller one, he might be more ambitious.

Lee, 31, Nyack, N.Y.

Her boyfriend moved to California and she went nuts because she couldn't afford to go see him. She got me to take up a collection in our building, because she figured that if everybody gave just two dollars, that would pay her way. She made me pretend she didn't have a clue about the collection, that it was a complete surprise. So I did this. I went around and collected $194, two dollars a pop. And then she met Jeff. Dumped the guy in California. And I had to return all $194, two dollars a pop.

Akela, 22, Washington, D.C.

She calls me when she fights with her husband. Sometimes right in the heat of battle. She tells me everything he does wrong, what she can't stand about him. The awful things he says when they fight. The names he calls her, the stuff he brings up from the past. I'm not there when they make up. I never hear about that. So, when I see him, they're all lovey-dovey, but I want to punch them both.

Penny, 33, Camden, Maine

She suspects every woman she sees of being after her husband. Not to burst her bubble, but I seriously doubt that anybody else would want the guy. I mean, it's not like anyone really *notices* him.

Carly, 23, Fort Worth, Tex.

197

Kim cried to me about her husband's affair for months. Now, they've made up and suddenly she acts like it never happened. And he never drank too much, either. And if I vaguely refer to anything he might ever have done to upset her, she gets mad at me. *I'm* the bad guy.

Leslie, 41, Tacoma, Wash.

We travel together, as couples, and they insist on getting adjacent or adjoining rooms. This is fine, except that her husband snores—I *assume* it's her husband—It *can't* be *her*. Anyway, the walls shake. The floors rattle. In the morning, we're exhausted; they've slept fine, feel spry as puppies, ready to boogie.

Ilene, 34, Cheyenne, Wyo.

She wanted to see if Ted was cheating on her, so we followed him after work one night. We waited in her car until she saw his car pull out of the lot and we tailed him. Clearly, he wasn't going home. He drove out of the city. About twenty miles, and the whole way, she's cursing him out, saying what a lying *@! cheat he is. Finally, he pulled over to get gas and, guess what? We've been following the wrong car. We'd been following a complete stranger who also drove a red Suzuki.

Gloria, 33, Philadelphia, Pa.

We used to be chicks. I mean, see-through bikinis, ambushing the lifeguards at the beach, the whole nine yards. We had one double date—it was a blind date. She liked the boy I was supposed to go out with better, so we switched. We pretended that she was me and I was her. The whole night, we went by each other's names. He thought her name was Lois, and when he called her to go out again, her mother had no idea why I was getting phone calls at her house. But she kept it up. They went out for a month or two before she told him who she was.

Lois, 41, Cherry Hill, N.J.

My husband and Phyllis pick on each other, swipe at each other. She'll say, "Ed, darling, you really need a shave." He'll say, "Phyllis, dear. Not half as bad as you do." They bicker like husband and wife.

Marilyn, 37, Santa Fe, N.Mex.

Sandra often asks me not to tell "anyone, even Phil." She's my best friend; Phil's my husband. So what she's doing is setting up a barrier between him and me. But then, she doesn't need him knowing all her secrets. And Phil doesn't like me telling Sandra our private business, either. So what happens is that I end up dividing myself into pieces that belong to him, pieces that belong to her, and pieces that belong to me, that don't need to have any part of either one of them.

Letitia, 27, Los Angeles, Calif.

Mavis wipes the floor with her husband. Treats him like a rag. I adore the guy. He tries to please her, but she never gives him the satisfaction of being pleased. She believes that in a marriage, one partner has to have the upper hand. If she gave him peace of mind, she thinks he wouldn't appreciate her any more. He'd take her for granted and treat her like she's treating him.

Flora, 37, Oshkosh, Wis.

Lily flirts with anything male. She flirts with my twelve-year-old son. Her son's seventeen. She flirts with his friends, offers them soft drinks and popcorn, chats, acts as if they come over to see her.

Roxie, 39, La Porte, Ind.

203

Every time we go over there, Mindy and her husband fight. Their teeth are clenched but they smile, call each other "Dear" and "Darling." He growls, "Why don't you serve the *soup*, DARLING?" She snarls, "Why don't you bring the *tureen*, SWEETHEART?" Their jaws are set. Their eyes sear each other's skin. If you join the conversation, you're in the middle. "Lil wants to know how I *am*, DARLING! Why don't *you* tell her how I *am* and, while you're at it, tell her *why* I'm this way, DEAR." It's tense, but a great floor show.

Lily, 34, Austin, Tex.

Debbie has a crush on my big brother. Always has. Since, maybe, fifth grade. She asks me how he is, how his business is doing, when he's going to visit. When he's around, I try not to include her or else she hangs on him, literally. She sits real close to him and tries to be seductive right in front of his wife. He thinks it's cute. He still sees her as a plump little kid, same way he sees me.

Jessica, 21, Tulsa, Okla.

She tells me more than I want to know about her husband. Like every time I look at him I think about how he brushes his teeth while he's peeing, to save time.

Chloe, 32, Indianapolis, Ind.

She has this gallows humor. When my boyfriend broke off our engagement, she phoned in his obituary to the local newspaper. She sent a sympathy card to his new girlfriend.

Leila, 24, Tampa, Fla.

If you judge what somebody thinks of you by who they fix you up with, Margie must think I'm pathetic—and totally desperate.

Laura, 29, Taos, N.Mex.

She's so identified with me that she has to experience whatever I do. In restaurants, she orders whatever I order. In college, she majored in the same field as I did, took the same courses, a semester behind me, even used my old books. She had her wisdom teeth pulled the day after I did. At my wedding, she seduced the best man. Hey, at least it wasn't the groom.

Bonnie, 20, Braintree, Mass.

I'm the reason she kept her virginity; she's the reason I lost mine. She figured, "If Ellen can be popular and still be a virgin, so can I." I figured, "If Gail can be respected and still sleep with her boyfriend, so can I." By the time we shared our assumptions about each other, of course, history had been written.

Ellen, 24, Seattle, Wash.

She's the horniest person I know. Sex is all she talks about. Everywhere we go, she's checking out the waiter, the lifeguard, the salesman, the cabdriver. Speculates about their private parts. She whispers, "Beefsteak. Hanging on the right."

Carolyn, 30, Boston, Mass.

We took vacations together, went to movies every Friday, brunch every Sunday. We worked out at our health club every other day, talked on the phone every night. Played tennis, hiked, cooked, went camping, to concerts—did everything together. Until she met Alex. Now, I'm a third wheel. Dumped. Out in the cold. Unwelcome, unwanted. Like a divorcée, only I get no alimony. After ten years, I've been fired. No retirement plan. Don't get me wrong—I'm happy for her. For them both. Truly, I am.

Carol, 31, Montgomery, Ala.

CHAPTER 6

MATERIAL GIRLS

"If She Weren't My Best Friend, I'd Kill Her!"

In even the most spiritual friendships, material issues inevitably arise. Lunch checks must be split, tips and tabs calculated, tickets, gifts, and parking paid for, gas tanks filled. Many tight friendships have been choked by even tighter pursestrings.

But, money aside, the world presents an endless array of potential treasures, baubles, trips, and toys, all of which can affect friendships. Stella says, "Carson married Walter the Millionaire, drives a Lexus, wears designer clothes, splashes his money around, and laughs about how poor she used to be—as if she doesn't notice that I still *am*."

No matter how much stuff we have, lose, or acquire, most of us agree that money can't buy love, that the best things in life are free. Still, even among friends, material disparities can cause distress, possessions can be powerful, cash can count, and money might matter. Or not, depending.

ita will not discuss money. It's like a nonsubject. She'll say she got a raise, but never how big. A bonus, but never how much. I told her how much my new job paid, and she looked at me like I'd pulled my pants down in public.

Maureen, 33, Dover, Del.

Allison never mentions money. Never asks a price. It's taboo. She nearly filleted me for asking a waiter how much the special was.

Adrianne, 37, Washington, D.C.

Gladys buys just what she needs and no more. Never an extra slice of bologna. If you drop by, she won't offer you a cracker. You have to ask for a glass of water, and she removes the glass the second you're done. There's nothing in her refrigerator. If you come to dinner, she serves one beverage and one portion of everything. One chicken thigh and an ear of corn. That's it. No seconds, no leftovers. She's very exact.

Jackie, 42, Louisville, Ky.

harlotte spends money easily, charges gobs of stuff she doesn't need and won't ever use, and she's never earned a dime. She gives clothes she's never worn to charity. She used to spend her dad's money; now she spends her husband's. She writes checks but never records them. When I asked her why, she shrugged, "Mort'll cover it."

Brenda, 29, Medford, N.J.

oing somewhere with Valerie is like a trip to *The Price Is Right*. She nudges me, points out objects, and announces how much she thinks they're worth. "Look—that coat cost ten thousand." Then she'll add, "But her pendant's glass, fifty dollars at most."

Libby, 52, Atlanta, Ga.

She admires my outfit, nags me until I tell her where I got it, and shows up the next day wearing the same thing in a different color. She thinks it's great if we happen to wear them to the same place. We look like Tweedledee and Tweedledum.

Lacey, 27, Raleigh, N.C.

She lies about bargains. She told me she got a great price on camping gear at a store way out in the western suburbs. So I drove there. Guess what? The store doesn't even carry that brand. They'd have to order it, and it would cost about four times the price she mentioned.

Tina, 27, Boston, Mass.

You'd never know she has an IQ of maybe 200, got straight A's in school, a scholarship to Barnard. All she can talk about is shopping. Bargains. Coupons. How much you can save on mustard, if you buy the economy size.

Ellyn, 30, Stamford, Conn.

Barbara Jean cannot resist a sale. She drags me all over the county to buy stuff she'd never look at except that it's reduced. And it's contagious. I end up buying things I don't need just because I'm there. "Look how much you saved!" she'll rave. "You got a great bargain on those coaster holders!"

Trudy, 38, Knoxville, Tenn.

She's an impulse buyer. She sees a vase, a tea set, an embroidered pillow and simply *has* to have it. When she gets home, she feels guilty for splurging on something she didn't need, so she skips lunch for a week to pay herself back. Basically, she never eats lunch.

Ruby, 44, San Jose, Calif.

She's kind of a scrooge. She buys gifts, but only practical ones. Like tennis balls for my birthday. Tupperware for Christmas. One Christmas she gave me a snow scraper. For her birthday, as a joke, I bought her a plunger. She loved it, thought it was a great gift idea.

Marlene, 28, Utica, N.Y.

Ida has to outdo me. Everything of hers has to be newer and more expensive than everything of mine. And she'll stoop to any low to do it. Our weddings were a month apart. She asked around to find out who was making my dress, went to see the dressmaker, and asked to see my gown. She told the dressmaker I'd told her to look at it "to get ideas" for her own gown. The dressmaker refused and told me what happened. Ida's never mentioned it.

Nancy, 26, Wayne, Pa.

Jayne orders six of everything on the menu; you order a small salad, and then she says, "Why don't we just split the bill, fifty-fifty?"

Candace, 29, Louisville, Ky.

work in a department store, and I sometimes let her use my discount. This is okay; after all, she's my best friend. But she uses it to buy *me* presents. My birthday gift, my Christmas presents. On my discount.

Christine, 29, Glenview, Ill.

Kelly never has any cash. No change for parking meters or soda machines. It's small stuff, so I feel petty asking for it. But, if I did, she wouldn't have the cash to pay me back, anyhow.

Summer, 22, Madison, Wis.

She assumes everyone's got money. She wants to go to the theater, to dinner at restaurants my husband and I can't afford. She wants me to join her tennis club. Money's just always been there for her. Shopping's a sport to her, something to fill her time. If she gets bored, she buys garden furniture, puts in a pool.

Tanya, 35, Lake Forest, Ill.

Patsy has to be the one to pay. She buys the movie tickets or picks up the lunch check every time. I feel uncomfortable about it, but she insists. I think it's a control thing.

Helen, 28, Denver, Colo.

She's great company but she's cheap. She never leaves a big enough tip, always leaves a dollar or two less than her share. And she'll never just divide a bill in half—she sits there and figures it out item by item, to the exact *penny*. And, somehow, her share is always less than mine.

Hilary, 28, New York, N.Y.

221

Penny wears a diamond on her finger that's the size of her head, but she'll short you on the tip.

Jessie, 34, Bowling Green, Ohio

She returns things for a refund after she uses them and tells the store that the stuff was defective. She returned a camera saying it didn't work, when really she'd dropped it on a concrete floor. She returned a chain saw after her husband finished chopping the dead tree—I don't know what excuse she used. But she was real proud of herself. She even pulled out a few threads so the silk looked damaged and then returned her wedding dress. "It cost over a thousand bucks," she said. "And Lord knows I'll never wear it again."

Peggy, 29, Dallas, Tex.

She uses full service at the gas station, never does anything herself. If she has to change a lightbulb, I bet she calls a handyman.

Freda, 49, De Kalb, Ill.

Holly must earn six figures; I struggle to pay my rent. I have no idea how she's succeeded so well. She's ambitious and aggressive, but not especially bright. She never gets jokes. And she doesn't think quickly. By the time she makes a comeback, the subject has changed three times.

Olivia, 35, Wilmington, Del.

The only requirement for Gail to like something is that it cost a lot. She thinks you can never wear too much jewelry, never have a brooch too big, never have too many designer labels. Her toilet would be gold-plated if she could only find one.

Marsha, 34, Dallas, Tex.

Whenever I go to her place, she's cleaning her jewelry. We sit around. I make a snack and watch TV; she soaks her diamonds.

Libby, 27, Philadelphia, Pa.

Whenever she goes away, Paula brings me the tackiest gift she can find. I've got seashell salt shakers, a lobster claw paperweight, a lobster claw headband. Pens with hula dancers that have disappearing bras. Snow falling on the Statue of Liberty. Mickey ears. She thinks these are serious souvenirs. I used to toss them, but now I keep them. Someday, I'll open a kitsch museum.

Margie, 32, Kansas City, Mo.

Michelle budgets very carefully. Each week, she deposits some money in the bank, divides the rest up among her envelopes. She has about forty of them. Each one's labeled: Groceries, Clothing, Entertainment, Christmas Gifts, Piano, Paris, and so on. When she has enough in the Piano envelope, she'll buy a piano. But if Christmas comes around and she needs more cash for gifts, she steals from another envelope. Money tends to migrate from envelope to envelope, and there never seems to be much in any of them.

Miranda, 31, Putnam, W.Va.

The woman's not rich, but she's got a big heart. She gives money to anyone who asks for it. Panhandlers included. She sends five dollars to everyone who sends her junk mail, another five to every charity she sees advertised on TV.

Lily, 41, New Orleans, La.

She tells me what she wants for her birthday, starting about two months before. It never costs less than $100. For my birthday, she always gives me something she can't afford. An imported cashmere sweater, a leather jacket. It's like a contest, to see who'll spend the most.

Amber, 24, Davenport, Iowa

Carla manages miracles on a real limited income. This summer they're going to Italy. She buys everything—even makes phone calls on their credit card and collects airline miles. She sews most of their clothes, knits incredible sweaters, bakes her own bread. She gardens, grows vegetables, berries, apples, and peaches. She composts her garbage, cans fruit, makes jam. She'd make Martha Stewart feel inadequate. And I'm no Martha Stewart.

Amina, 30, Escondido, Calif.

She composts everything. This is good for the environment. But do not go in the backyard. Especially not on a hot day.

Lucille, 43, Shelbyville, Tenn.

Faye is forever making up businesses for us to go into. Not just pet-sitting and shopping for people. She wants us to make people's angry phone calls for them. Or write their angry letters. She called that one "A Page of Rage, Inc." Oh, and her "Fish-a-gram" business, where we'd deliver goldfish in bowls with red ribbons to executives. She actually bought a hundred goldfish for that one, but they were dead before we had any customers.

Angela, 38, Upper Darby, Pa.

My husband was out of work for a year, so we're heavily in debt. Alexis didn't tell me that she's going to Hawaii for her anniversary or show me her new emerald ring, because she didn't want to rub it in. She brings casseroles and meatloafs when she comes over, and invites us to Sunday dinner. She gives me coupons for cereal. I'm so embarrassed. We've been friends since kindergarten, but because of who we've married, we live in different worlds. She spends her time doing charity work, and I'm one of her charities.

MaryBeth, 32, Elmira, N.Y.

You can bet that she spends more on the wrapping than the gifts. And the wrapping's usually more useful. And don't try to return anything—the box may say Nordstroms, but, trust me, it's a blue-light special.

Marilyn, 38, Deerfield, Ill.

*A*bout three years ago, she hired my husband to handle this lawsuit she was involved in. He saved her a fortune, performed legal miracles for her, worked his butt off because she's my friend. But, because we're friends, she sees no reason to compensate him. She thinks he should have done whatever she needed for the sake of friendship. I told her we can't pay the grocer or the mortgage with friendship. So she pays him twenty dollars a month, and complains about it twenty times a day.

Sarah, 35, Topeka, Kans.

When she buys gifts, she signs my name to the cards. I get thanked for things I never knew I gave people, and then she asks me for $20 or $30 to cover my half. She never asks; she just does it. It doesn't occur to her to ask if I like what she's bought. Or if I think it's too pricey. Or if I've already bought the person something else.

Samantha, 27, Baltimore, Md.

She can't hold on to inanimate objects. She loses stuff. Sweaters, jackets, hats, keys, sunglasses. Whatever. Every time she comes over, she leaves something. Comes back for her scarf, leaves a glove. Comes back for the glove, leaves her purse.

April, 31, Taos, N.Mex.

233

Doreen swears by coupons. She says she saved three dollars and seventy-five cents last week. Four dollars and thirty-five cents this week. In a year, she says she saves a couple hundred bucks. And spends just as many hours searching for coupons, cutting them out, and sorting through them at the check-out counter.

Erin, 29, Milwaukee, Wis.

She collects African art, has about nine fertility statues in her apartment. Big ones, small ones. I seriously feel uncomfortable going to her place—I got pregnant with twins not long after my first visit there.

Shelley, 33, Los Angeles, Calif.

She collects dolls. Antiques, porcelain, clowns, rag dolls, corn-husk dolls, baby dolls. Puppets, dummies. They're everywhere. On shelves, in cases, on furniture. I don't want to hurt her feelings, but they scare the hell out of me.

Adrienne, 33, Louisville, Ky.

Her apartment's furnished in early Addams Family. She buys everything secondhand, often at estate sales. Her furniture, clothes, accessories. Dishes. It doesn't bother her that she's eating off some dead guy's plates or walking in the shoes of a dead woman. She says it's good to recycle.

April, 24, Omaha, Nebr.

If there were an Ugly Shoes Contest, she'd win. If they're ugly, she'll buy them. Her outfits are fine, normal, usually real cute. But her feet wear a completely different wardrobe. They're like separate characters altogether.

Holly, 23, Albuquerque, N.Mex.

Margaret cannot resist shoes. She buys a new pair whenever she goes shopping. She never wears most of them—there aren't enough days in the year. She couldn't possibly. She has a closetful. I thought about reading up on the shoe fetish thing. But I decided that maybe I don't want to know.

Pamela, 40, Larchmont, N.Y.

Marsha's in a constant state of redoing her apartment. She can't afford to redecorate, so mostly she rearranges. Mirrors and wall hangings trade places; the TV is never where you watched it last time. It's best to look behind you; the chair might move before you can sit down.

Debra, 23, Springfield, Mass.

She uses an interior decorator. Pays a fortune to have the most ostentatious, overstated, glitziest home I've ever seen. Her bedroom's papered in huge red, silver, and gold flowers, even on the ceiling. The furniture—even the bed frame—is red formica and chrome. The sunken living room's papered in blue, silver, and gold diagonal stripes, even on the ceiling. There's a grey and blue zigzag-striped sectional sofa, black and blue rectangles on a white carpet. The whole house is like that. Nothing's peaceful. The powder room's lime green, silver, and yellow swirls. I get a headache when I go there.

Dawn, 38, Scarsdale, N.Y.

She intends to recycle, so she collects empty yogurt cups in her basement. Her basement's full of plastic containers and tin cans, old soda bottles. By full, I mean ankle-deep.

Stella, 33, Amherst, N.Y.

Colleen has her entire childhood in her guest room. Old dolls and stuffed animals, photographs, posters, books. Record albums and tapes. Postcards people sent her. Her princess phone. It was all at her mother's until she threatened to throw it out. So she furnished her spare room in Early Colleen. It's very nostalgic. When I step in there, I want to be a twelve-year-old again, flop on the floor and listen to the Beatles till Mom calls me home for dinner.

Bev, 38, Minneapolis, Minn.

Shoes are very important to her. She sizes people up by their shoes. How shiny or scuffed-up they are. The style, the quality, the material or leather. Whether they're comfortable or fashionable. She can identify imports, often even the manufacturers. And she thinks she can tell a person's personality by what they wear on their feet. I prefer to go barefoot, whenever I can. What does *that* tell her?

Heather, 27, Dallas, Tex.

FUN

"If She Weren't My Best Friend, I'd Kill Her!"

Fun may be the glue that holds friends together, bonding them with good times, private jokes, and precious memories. But exactly what *is* "fun"? The definition changes with fads, phases, ages, trends, times, tides, and momentary moods. What's "fun" for one person can, therefore, be torture for another.

"Gloria insists that I go to the shore with her," Lydia complains. "I sit under a hat and an umbrella wearing long sleeves and number 50 sunblock getting sand in my swimsuit. She body surfs, makes sand castles. On the way home, she says, 'Now, wasn't that just the *greatest?*'"

Good friends share and share alike, celebrating whenever, wherever, and whatever they can. And so, with the best of intentions, we generously include our friends in our good times, involving them in the activities that please us most, whether they like it or not. And *that* is what we call "fun."

un, according to Peggy, is relative to money. You measure your good time by how much got spent on you. Unless you're paying your own way, then it's how much you saved. Discounts, coupons, checks you got someone else to pick up.

Janice, 26, Dallas, Tex.

For Alyssa, fun has to involve food. Preferably chocolate.

Bev, 37, Evanston, Ill.

Fun isn't fun without men. Or the potential of men. According to Tracey, everything else is a waste of time.

Stephanie, 25, Richmond, Va.

Eating out is her favorite thing to do. Someplace expensive. With someone else paying.

Jessica, 22, Bethesda, Md.

Fun, for Evie, has to be fattening.

Dolly, 31, Portland, Maine

The thing she likes most is playing bridge. Second to that, she likes talking about playing bridge. Then comes reading about bridge, thinking up strategies for playing bridge . . . you get the idea.

Myrtle, 67, Sarasota, Fla.

Shopping is all Audrey ever wants to do. Anything else is bogus.

Sondra, 21, Dallas, Tex.

Myra adopts a completely different personality when she plays bridge. She's a sociopath. A killer with no conscience. Her face changes, becomes stony and brutal. She shows no mercy, no kindness whatsoever. I don't mean just for her opponents—I mean for her *partner*. Who is usually me.

Edith, 57, Wilmington, Del.

All Trudy ever wants to do is watch TV. She hates to miss an episode of *Frasier*. Plans her social calendar around the TV listings. On a big night she might rent a tape.

Georgia, 39, Norman, Okla.

247

Bubble baths. She eats bonbons, reads romances, talks on the phone in the tub. She has a pillow there so her back won't hurt. All she wants to do is soak.

Naomi, 33, St. Cloud, Minn.

Miranda sees phallic symbols everywhere. Not just in certain vegetables or national monuments. I'm talking about streetlights, loaves of bread, cigars, pens, motorcycles. Tailpipes. Buses. Skyscrapers. Skis. It's gotten so I can't look at anything without seeing the "symbol."

Lois, 39, Milwaukee, Wis.

he likes line dancing.

Wanda, 27, Pittsburgh, Pa.

leeping is her ideal, favorite activity. She never wants to go anywhere, do anything that will interfere with her sleep, and insists on being home by eleven, no matter how good a party is. Give her three wishes and they'd be: To go to sleep early, to sleep late, and to go back to bed again after breakfast.

Cindy, 26, Columbus, Ohio

he writes poetry. And reads it aloud.

Ashley, 25, Richmond, Va.

249

Ilana reads. She would be content to see no one and go nowhere, if she could have an endless supply of books.

Toni, 21, Dover, Del.

Lorrie loves to get dressed up for a formal wedding or party where men wear tuxedos and she wears a gown. And she can dance with elegant strangers, sip champagne, and act like she's somebody she absolutely normally isn't. She enjoys trying on different personae, putting on airs. It's a Cinderella thing.

Pat, 33, New Orleans, La.

She will spend hours, literally, combing the sand for shells. This is truly a compulsion. Once she gets into it, you can't stop her. Like what, is she surprised to find shells at the shore? Does she hope to find diamond rings?

Jennie, 23, Flemington, N.J.

251

Everywhere Lois goes ends up being a sitcom. Even a funeral. The brother of one of our classmates died of a sudden heart attack. It was terrible. Literally hundreds of people attended the funeral. We were near the rear of the endless line of cars going to the cemetery. It was a long drive, and Lois had missed breakfast. So, when we passed a Burger King, she pulled out of the line to get a hamburger. You guessed it: The rest of the funeral procession followed her, right through the takeout line. She bought milkshakes for the next ten cars. And she got them there in time for the burial.

Liz, 33, Atlanta, Ga.

She does math in her head. For fun. While you're driving she figures out how much the gas'll cost, the average miles per gallon, the time it will take to drive to Jacksonville, if you go five miles above the speed limit all the way.

Pam, 25, Lexington, Ky.

She obsesses on crossword puzzles. She calls me for help when she gets stuck. Once she called me at midnight to ask me if I knew a five-letter word that means happiness. I said, "S-L-E-E-P."

Delta, 37, Knoxville, Tenn.

She tries on clothes and jewelry. She can do this all day, going from store to store. Doesn't spend a dime.

Abby, 23, San Jose, Calif.

TJ insists that I be her tennis partner. Then she spends the whole time yelling at me. She criticizes my position, foot work, followthrough. I'm lunging for the ball and she yells, *"Run! Get it! Remember to follow through!"* Which totally distracts me so I miss it, and then she yells at me for not keeping my eye on the ball.

Weather, 37, Anaheim, Calif.

Jasmine has a two-bedroom apartment. One of the bedrooms is for the birds. I mean, literally. She keeps birds in there. Uncaged, so they can "feel free." No furniture, just newspaper on the floor. She loves them to sit on her head, her shoulders. She feeds them from her mouth. If you open the door, they sweep at your head like in the Hitchcock movie.

Leilah, 23, Binghamton, N.Y.

Nothing interferes with her tennis game. Nothing. If the Grim Reaper wants her, he'll have to wait till she finishes the point.

Lois, 41, Evanston, Ill.

255

She's a compulsive surfer. She spends hours at the computer. Meantime, her apartment's a mess. Her hair isn't brushed. But she hasn't got time to clean or cook or do mundane things like laundry. She's got to ride the Net.

Phoebe, 26, Sterling Heights, Mich.

Pat convinced me to drive out to the mountains and go camping with her. It began to rain. I mean, a torrential downpour. We were out in the middle of nowhere in a dark, wind-howling storm, and the stakes of the tent slipped out of the mud, and the whole thing collapsed on our heads. To climb out, we had to push wads of tent out of our faces and feel around to find the zipper. When I finally got out, I slipped and sat in the mud, pummeled by ice cold rain, and promised Pat that she would not live to see the end of the storm. Finally, we stuffed the whole mess in the back of my car and drove back, four and a half hours. This was two years ago, and you can still see mud smears in the backseat of my car. She wants me to try it again.

Faye, 28, Indianapolis, Ind.

She can't have fun unless she does something perfectly. Or at least better than everyone else. Whatever it is—bowling, gambling, cooking, shopping— she has to be the ace. And I'm sure that the "being better" part is more fun to her than the activity itself.

Melanie, 48, Lindenwold, N.J.

Gum's a musical instrument in Georgia's mouth. She doesn't just crack it. She produces whole ranges of tone and rhythm.

Lee, 24, Parma, Ohio

She enjoys body functions, scatological humor. Belches like a construction worker. Her favorite jokes are about passing gas, and she has a million of them.

Eleanor, 24, Detroit, Mich.

Lindsey gets kicks out of doing stuff she knows she shouldn't. Even simple things like eating junk food. But she's just as likely to bungee jump or shave half her head and dye the rest green. Or pierce parts of her body that you can't normally see. She'll do anything on a dare.

Denise, 21, New York, N.Y.

We were in a restaurant, eating. Something went down the wrong pipe and I started coughing. Suddenly, Sue jumps up, runs around the table, knocking over a chair and a bottle of wine, and she grabs me, drags me half out of my chair and starts giving me the Heimlich maneuver. I knock my plate into my lap, wrestling to get her off of me. The harder I resist her, the harder she squeezes. She practically killed me. She still won't believe that a person can't scream and choke at the same time. She's convinced she saved my life. "You owe me," she says.

Rebecca, 34, Amherst, Mass.

Knock-knock jokes. She thinks they're hysterical. She won't let up, so you have to give in and ask, "Who's there?" The dumber they are, the more she likes them. She gets them from her four- and six-year-old kids, and passes them along. Till you seriously threaten to knock-knock her head.

Gabriella, 27, Allentown, Pa.

Gena picks at herself. She's always picking at something. At the beach, it's her feet. But if she can't get to them, she'll pick at a pimple, cuticles, a hangnail, chapped lips, a patch of dry skin. Oh, and if she has a *scab,* she's in heaven.

Lacey, 23, Buffalo, N.Y.

261

She still sunbathes, by the hour. Bikini, radio, bad novels, the whole bit. Except now she doesn't use a reflector or baby oil; she uses number 15. That's her only concession to the times.

Melanie, 34, Miller, Ind.

Claire spends hours caring for her hair. She calls it "virgin hair," uses baby shampoo and conditioner, and brushes it a hundred strokes twice a day. Every day. If she gets interrupted or loses count, she starts over.

Alice, 31, Tampa, Fla.

Paula lives to clean. She cleans *under* the cushions of the sofa. Her floor's so clean, it's slippery. Her refrigerator sparkles. There's not a fingerprint on the handle. Ever. The woman *vacuums* for pleasure.

Sue, 44, Providence, R.I.

263

o not let her have a drink. She might do anything. Say anything. Use the wrong word. Spill all over herself. Pee in her pants. Kiss someone else's husband. Curse. Have a laughing fit. Tell people what she really thinks of them. I've seen it all.

Darcy, 25, Toms River, N.J.

he adores movies. She spends hours—days— discussing every line, scene, character, symbol. Not to mention every costume, set design, and special effect. And the personal careers and love lives of every actor or actress in the show. And which of the male actors' love lives she'd like to enhance.

Sarah, 32, New York, N.Y.

She loves Frank Sinatra. Plays his tapes all the time. At home. In the car. She sings along. Dances if she can.

Maria, 49, St. Louis, Mo.

She blames me for being allergic to her cat, can't understand that allergies aren't a matter of choice. When she gave me a wedding shower, she locked the cat in the bedroom, but after about ten minutes, I was wheezing and sneezing. My eyes were red and tearing, my nose streaming. She was mad at me for *months* for leaving early.

Donna, 30, Elgin, Ill.

265

Jennifer loves her dog. It's this ratty little terrier with bows in its hair that snaps at you if you try to pet it and growls if you get between it and Jennifer. She wants it with her all the time, takes it everywhere.

Kathy, 37, Los Angeles, Calif.

Louise's dog pees on my stuff. My coat, my bag. My boots. It's a little thing, one of those pugs. She says it's in love with me. That peeing on my stuff means he's marking me as his territory. That I should be flattered. I tell her I adore her, so would it be okay if I pee on her purse? She laughs.

Noelle, 40, Chicago, Ill.

She has this French poodle. Which she adores. It smells. It jumps on me, claws me, slimes me with its tongue. It sniffs my crotch. If I sit down, it humps my leg.

Ruth, 29, Des Plaines, Ill.

She leaves her cats with me every time she goes away, which is, basically, every holiday. They tear up my Christmas tinsel and claw my furniture. At night, they climb onto my bed, sleep on my face, or pounce on me at five A.M. They howl in the middle of the night. But she can't bear to leave them with anyone but me.

Carla, 32, Boise, Idaho

267

She's into taxidermy. She has all her old pets stuffed and sitting around the house. She pats Rex on the head, talks to Puffy and Snowflake as if they were still alive. If I die before she does, I've made my family swear not to let her near me.

Evelyn, 58, Kenosha, Wis.

Maryann can't resist cats. She has seven. They sleep with her, make themselves at home on your coat, rub against your legs. She smells of them. Sometimes, I swear, she looks like them.

Flora, 33, Madison, Wis.

Nan's a do-it-yourselfer. She changes the oil in her car, mows her own grass, paints her bedroom, tiles her floors. Anyone who won't snake her own toilet's a princess. She doesn't understand that not everyone feels passionate about duct cleaning or chimney flashing.

Rosemarie, 38, Nashville, Tenn.

She's obsessed with, fascinated by, probably in love with death. Any occasion—New Year's, Christmas, her birthday, her kids' birthdays—*any* milestone's a sign that our lives are passing, that death is that much closer. At her son's kindergarten graduation, she dried her eyes and sighed, "Life is going so quickly. Soon he'll be an old man, and you and I will be rotting in our graves."

Beth, 31, Richmond, Va.

Bonita loves to speak French. In restaurants, she orders in French and the waiters have no idea what she's saying. I "translate."

Mia, 25, Wilmington, Del.

She loves oldies and sings them with great enthusiasm. Except she sings the wrong words. "My Boyfriend's Back," she actually thinks is, "My Boyfriend's Black." To her, "Hang on, Sloopy," is "Hang on, Stupid." In Credence Clearwater Revival's "Bad Moon Rising," "bad moon on the rise," is "the bathroom on the right." In, "Will You Still Love Me Tomorrow?" there's a line, "Can I believe the magic of your sighs?" She sings, "the magic of your thighs." I told her it was "sighs," not "thighs." She said, "Oh. *I* get it. He's *big.*"

Lacey, 39, Nashville, Tenn.

271

I left my dog with her when I went to Mexico. I didn't know him when I came back. She'd had him shaved, so he looked like some bush in a formal garden. With bows in his fur.

Stephanie, 28, Shreveport, La.

She loves tragedies. Sees herself as a tragic figure. Contemplates what might have been, what never will be, who she might have loved, what she might have achieved had she taken a different path. As far as I can see, the one great tragedy of her life is that she's tone deaf and doesn't know it. Her singing. Now, *that's* truly tragic.

Terri, 23, Greeley, Colo.

Whenever we go anywhere, Ethel brings a can of spray disinfectant in case she needs to use a bathroom. She also carries antibacterial wipes so she can "keep her hands clean."

Bobbi, 62, Hartford, Conn.

When we go on trips, she wants to see every sight, museum, birthplace, relic. She wakes up with an itinerary and schedule, a plan we have to stick to. When we go on trips, I want to eat every food, lie on every beach. Turn over occasionally. We have different goals, but still end up taking vacations together, so one or the other of us is always griping.

Jane, 26, Pittsburgh, Pa.

273

We save all year to go on vacation, pick a destination and go together. I should say, we're together until she meets a man. Then I'm on my own.

Phyllis, 47, Baltimore, Md.

Our families bought a summer home together. I didn't think this through sufficiently. Every time I go up there, there's some atrocity added to the decor. Awful curtains, light fixtures so ugly they're frightening. She picked up a smelly old loveseat at a garage sale; you sneeze if you sit on it. And she asked me for half of the money. Oh, and they just got a puppy. A St. Bernard puppy.

Carole, 39, Charlotte, N.C.

She loves clichés, always has some dumb line to apply to a situation, but she doesn't say the whole line. Just key phrases. "Silver linings." "Honey and vinegar." "Spilt milk." "Cookie crumbles." "Save nine." You get the idea.

Meg, 31, Atlanta, Ga.

She's not evil, she's absent minded. Once, we were shopping. I was in the fitting room, trying on outfits, and she's holding my clothes for me. I ask her to bring me a different size skirt, so she goes to get it and meantime remembers she has to put money in the meter. So she rushes out to the street, still holding my clothes and the too-small skirt, and gets stopped by a store detective for trying to steal the skirt. It took her half an hour to explain things to him and, meantime, I'm stuck in the fitting room in my underwear.

Barb, 23, St. Louis, Mo.

For Annie, life is fun, fun is life. Whatever happens, she sees it in terms of fun, can't respond in any other way. When I found a lump in my breast, she said that a mastectomy would give me a great opportunity to get my whole body sculpted. To remake myself into a 10. And party on.

Joie, 39, Washington, D.C.

The '60s? She has no idea they're over. She's a hippie, wears her grey hair long and straight, lots of beads. Loose, flowy dresses. She listens to Bob Dylan, the Stones, and the Beatles. At stoplights, she flashes the peace sign to drivers in neighboring cars.

Priscilla, 50, Boston, Mass.

Peg makes me get off my duff and do things. This is good. Because of her I've learned to play golf, ride horses, and taken up cross-country skiing. If she didn't drag me with her, I'd spend my spare time on my sofa, reading, watching the tube, munching junk food. Life would be more dull, but easier. And much less expensive.

Benita, 38, Rochester, Maine

She loves practical jokes. For my bridal shower, she baked "funny" brownies. Aunt Vera fell asleep and snored all through the party; my mother and Aunt Rose giggled and ate all the leftovers.

Lottie, 26, Philadelphia, Pa.

She loves making plans. Figuring out what we'll do in optimum and least favorable conditions. If we're going to, say, a movie, she'll plan a time to meet, based on her calculations of how long it takes to drive there, the possibility of heavy traffic, parking, ticket lines, popcorn lines, and time to go to the ladies' room. And she'll have alternate plans, in case something goes wrong. "Always have a 'Plan B,'" she says.

Lil, 33, Arlington Heights, Ill.

nitting. That, to her, is a good time.

Candace, 30, Rock Springs, Wyo.

Her plants are like children to her. She names them, talks to them. Her garden's weedless and perfect. She coddles her rhododendron. Grows things I can't pronounce, treats them better than she treats most people.

Lorna, 36, Selma, Ala.

She gets great pleasure out of telling me to cheer up. She loves reminding me that, compared to starving strangers in some remote part of Asia or Africa, I don't have it so bad. That, in the course of geologic time, I'm so miniscule that I might as well not exist. That basically, I'm only bummed out because I'm too self-centered and egocentric to see how trivial my problems are.

Betsy, 31, Omaha, Nebr.

For Felicia, complaining is an art form. And she's an artist.

Vicki, 28, Telluride, Colo.

281

However tiny and helpless they are, babies change everything. Children alter women's priorities, loyalties, activities, and proclivities, and limit the amount of time, energy, and attention available for friends.

Friendships that have survived countless conflicts, romances, and careers can be confounded by a tiny infant. On the other hand, women who never had anything in common before find soul mates while pushing strollers or attending play groups.

"I met Carol at the park," Amy recalls. "We talked while our kids chalked up miles on the swings. That was my life—pushing and talking, talking and pushing. For years, aside from my husband, as far as adult contact went—she was it."

Once kids appear, women turn their attention from wine tasting to grapejuice staining, from politics to potty training, from literature to Little League. But just as the demands and constraints of parenting strain many a friendship, the support and rapport of friendships sustain many parents. Friends remind us that there is life beyond laundry. Or that, even if we're buried in Beanie Babies and lost in Legos, we are not alone.

All she does is yell. She yells at them to take baths, make their beds, not to spill, or track in mud. She also yells at them to eat their dinners, get a cookie. Give her a hug. Kiss her goodnight.

Mona, 36, South Bend, Ind.

When she had her baby, it took her husband a while to get there. So I was there with her for the first eleven hours of labor. She cursed at me and raised hell so bad that if he hadn't come when he did, I'd have pulled the little sucker out of her and gone home, put all of us out of our misery.

Coco, 24, Eugene, Oreg.

She named her kids after mine. I had Sarah; a year later, she had a girl and named her Sarah. Two months after I gave birth to Eric, she had a girl and named her Erica. This time, she's due seven months before I am. I guess she's going to wait seven months to name the baby.

Heather, 32, Corpus Christi, Tex.

ngela and her husband have trouble getting
pregnant. They're trying artificial insemination. It's all
they talk about. The whole neighborhood hears what
her temperature was that morning, when it indicated
that she was ovulating, how high his sperm count
was, what the motility was. How long it took him to
ejaculate into the cup. What magazines he used, which
centerfold turned him on this month.

Peggy, 35, Colorado Springs, Colo.

lyssa is ambitious for her children. It is a
serious matter to her if they score at a Peewee soccer
game. And more serious if they don't.

Sharon, 34, Merion, Pa.

aith never says anything good about her kids. She won't let you compliment them. If you say, "Little Sally looks beautiful." She'll say, "No. She needs a haircut." She's afraid the Evil Eye is watching. Or listening. I'm not sure what it is or how it works, but she doesn't want to mess with it.

Kelly, 31, Fort Myers, Fla.

arol feels free to correct my kids. She'll tell them not to interrupt, or to be quiet, to clear the table, to keep their hands to themselves. She'll tell them to stop whining. I mean, they're *my* kids, and I'm right there, their mother. But *she* feels called upon to discipline them.

Diane, 37, Dover, Del.

287

I make it a point to compliment her kids. I tell her how beautiful and polite, or how bright they are. I tell her they're delightful and growing so well. She accepts these compliments, agrees with and embellishes them. But she never, *ever* says a kind *word* about my children. Not one phrase. Not a single syllable. I keep waiting. I hint around. I mention their names, even. But she's mum. Will not say a thing.

Paloma, 34, Waukegan, Ill.

She does not censor herself or her language for the benefit of children. My kids have learned a lot from her. Let's just leave it at that.

Vanessa, 32, Omaha, Nebr.

Elaine yells at my kids like they're her own.

Cindy, 32, St. Charles, Ill.

She consulted a natal astrologist about when to conceive. About what would be the best month to deliver a child compatible to her and her husband. About which hemisphere, longitude, and latitude would create the most favorable conditions for conception. And, at the designated time, they went to the designated location, someplace in Ecuador, and conceived the ultimate, most astrologically advantaged child under the stars. Billy only *seems* like a normal, average kid.

Leslie, 36, Taos, N.Mex.

Suzanna does not discipline her kids. She never says, "No," so they have free rein. Last time she was at my house, one of them jumped on my bed for forty minutes. Truly. Meanwhile, her toddler repeatedly took a tape in and out of my VCR, and her seven-year-old decided to bathe Penny, my cat. He chased her until I finally picked her up and carried her around with me. They have no limits. Suzanna sits there, in the midst of pandemonium, continuing the conversation as if nothing's wrong. I clutch Penny and hold my breath, waiting for the next crash.

Cassy, 28, Austin, Tex.

Devon moans to *me* that her little Robby only got a "B" in math. She asks me if she should get him a special math tutor. Meantime, she knows I'd do a dance up Main Street if my Joel could get a "B" in math. A "B" in *anything*.

Barbara, 33, Green Bay, Wis.

291

Allison's four-year-old's behavior is erratic. When she comes over, she rearranges my furniture to clear a space for him, removes the coffee table and all breakables, and lets him wreak havoc. We can't talk or pay attention to anything but him. He's liable to hurt himself or something else, literally climbing the bookshelves, leaping over the upholstery. Her whole life is devoted to anticipating the trouble he can get into and trying to avoid it. But never to restraining him. Never telling him, "No."

Lydia, 34, Cameron, La.

She steals my babysitters. I find them, she meets them at my house, and they end up working for her.

Valerie, 33, Kenosha, Wis.

She never leaves her kids home. Never gets a baby-sitter. They can have runny noses, fevers, but they go out shopping with us. They can be misbehaving, whining, out of control, but they come along to lunch. And two days after I see them, like clockwork, my nose starts running.

Nicole, 32, Santa Fe, N.Mex.

Irene spends her life carting her kids from team to team, practice to practice, game to game. Her weekends are the worst—there can be three or four games on a single Saturday, since she has three boys. She calls me from the car to tell me she's too rushed to talk.

Betsy, 38, Tucson, Ariz.

293

She spoils my kids. When she's around, they avoid me. They ask her permission to do whatever they want, and she never tells them, "No." She never even says, "Ask your mom." It never occurs to her that I might take exception to this. Or that there are limits. We're talking ice cream sundaes before dinner. We're talking going out to play before homework's done. We're talking anarchy.

Lynelle, 34, Tacoma, Wash.

She talks about her kids' personal problems as if they're public entertainment. I used to hear about each sensual emanation Gillian made on the toilet. Now I know all her tampon stories.

294

Greta, 39, Winston-Salem, N.C.

She explains me to my kids. She apologizes to them for me. I say, "No. You can't have marshmallow topping for breakfast." She says, "Your mommy doesn't mean to be bossy. She just wants you to learn good eating habits, so when you grow up you won't have thighs like mine." I say, "Put away your stuff." She says, "Your mommy just wants to see who can pick up the most the fastest. I bet I can—I'll get the Legos!" And they're off. It's a game. She makes me sound like an ogre. I'm the Mean Old Mother and she's their fun-loving, patient, understanding Auntie.

Kate, 31, Green Bay, Wis.

When Tanya calls me, she lets her two-year-old grab the phone and babble for ten minutes while she does something else. She laughs, thinks it's cute that little Cecily likes to chat.

Emma, 30, New Haven, Conn.

Annie won't go anywhere without her baby. I mean, anywhere. So we don't go anywhere the baby can't. We eat at delis instead of restaurants; go to the playground instead of the orchestra. Instead of talking, we listen to him babble. Instead of eating, we watch him drool oatmeal. I watch her change diapers, do antics and acrobatics to make him smile. She's not interested in anything else but him. I miss her.

Maggie, 25, New York, N.Y.

Her son's six foot three, sixteen years old, and weighs about 300 pounds. She calls him, "My little monkey."

Evelyn, 39, Waukegan, Ill.

Rita reads every article and book she can find about anorexia, bulimia, Attention Deficit Disorder, drugs, teen pregnancy, AIDS, runaways, stress burnout, low self-esteem, acne—everything that can possibly happen to kids. She warns me to examine my kids for early warning signs of whatever she's reading about.

Marcie, 37, Richmond, Va.

My kids can't stand her kids, which is awkward because she's always trying to get us to go places as families. Or to make plans for the kids to get together. Have sleep-overs. My kids would rather sleep at the dentist's. It's bad.

Beth, 39, Winnetka, Ill.

Her daughter Regina gave my kids head lice. She said it was no big deal; Regina's whole class had them. I had to wash coats, hats, scarves, blankets, linens, pillows, stuffed animals, not to mention the shampoos and combing the damned things out of their heads. And every time my head itched for the next three weeks, I'd run to the mirror to check my hair. But it was "no big deal."

Jane, 29, Medford, N.J.

She gives my kids candy, cake, cookies, ice cream. Cotton candy. When I object, she declares, "I'm their aunt. I can spoil them." Meantime, I'm seething. Is she blind or sadistic? They're turning into serious tubs.

MaryBeth, 40, Winston-Salem, N.C.

299

She wants to think that our kids are interchangeable, the same in every way. But mine are sweeter. Better behaved. And prettier. And it makes me bristle when she lumps them together as if they're identical. "Boy, are they going to be impossible adolescents." "They're so fresh." "All they want to eat is pizza and all they want to do is watch TV." It's no use correcting her. If I say my kids prefer chicken and love salads, she says hers do, too, come to think of it.

Linda, 33, Cheyenne, Wyo.

Opal's son got his driver's license and now he takes off with my son, who's five months younger. I don't know where they are, when they're coming home, who they're with. She says, "Relax. You've got to trust them." Hello? We're dealing with teenagers, here. What's "trust" got to do with anything?

Jasmine, 36, Dallas, Tex.

She thinks her kids are precocious. I think they're monsters. They address adults as peers, by their first names. They participate in conversations not concerning them. Her son even corrects my speech. He interrupts, "You don't mean 'imply,' Ginny; you mean 'infer.'" She beams, "Very good, Keith."

Ginny, 37, Anaheim, Calif.

301

I have three girls. She has a boy and a girl. She loves to talk about how fulfilling it is to be the mother of a male. A future man. The yin and yang thing. Then she apologizes, as if I'm deprived. When I assure her I love my kids just the way they are, that I feel blessed and don't feel the need for a boy, she doesn't believe me. She empathizes, "Sure. Of course you'd have to feel that way."

Hope, 29, Selma, Ala.

She loves her cats, calls them her "babies." I'm supposed to feel honored that the oldest one's named after me. She's told me I'm its godmother.

Sally, 28, Twin Falls, Idaho

All she talks about is her kids. All she does is her kids. If any other subject comes up, she drops out. She feels out of touch with other topics. But she can't imagine why anyone would care to talk about anything besides her kids, anyway.

Marla, 31, Amherst, Mass.

She has no kids. If I mention mine, she yawns, "Please, Martha. *Tell* me you're not becoming one of those *boring* types who define themselves through motherhood!" So my kids are a non-topic. But they think she's odd because she talks to them like they're small adults, and that grosses them out. Like, she asked my fourteen-year-old if she's fallen in love yet. Said, "Well, when you do, let me know what you think of it."

Martha, 39, New Orleans, La.

She mooches off my sitters. She knows Betty's here watching the baby, so she offers her a few extra dollars to watch her kids, too. I come home and find a day care center.

Lynda, 31, Naples, Fla.

Her kids interrupt constantly. They pick up the phone to ask her questions, and she answers them, converses with them while you wait. If you're at her house, she'll walk away from you to discuss her daughter's choice of scrunchies or what they're having for dinner, or what tape they want to rent next weekend, what Mike said to Christie, what Christie said to Mike, what they want for Christmas, whatever. You sit there like, what am I doing here?

June, 34, Wilmington, Del.

She has rules about everything, about what they can or can't eat, spend, watch on TV, read about. Rules about where they can or can't go. Games they can or can't play. It's not like this for my kids, so it's hard. My kids will eat candy; hers will stare at them longingly, aching for a bite.

Sandy, 34, Knoxville, Tenn.

About five years ago, I left my hamsters with her when I had to go out of town. They died. A few years later, I asked her to take care of my tropical fish while I was away. They died. Now, my husband and I have to go to New York for the weekend. She wants to watch my son.

Phyllis, 31, Randolph, Vt.

She calls my son "Junior." Never Rick, Rich, Richie, Ricky, Dick, or Richard. No. She calls him "Junior." He doesn't like it, but I tell him not to complain; at least she's stopped calling him "Sweetie Pie."

Miranda, 38, Baltimore, Md.

You can't call her son "Billy" or "Bill" or even "Will." She'll scold you. "He's William," she'll say. And Alexandra can't be "Alex" or "Allie." She'll also scold you if you call them pet names like Sweetheart, Shortstuff. Pal. Honey. Buddy. "That's so condescending." You've got to call them as she named them, articulate the whole nine yards.

Lisa, 30, Philadelphia, Pa.

She gives me her kids' tattered old clothes, toys. Things you'd be embarrassed to give to charity. A sweatshirt with her daughter's name embroidered in sequins. Like my Claire should wear a sweatshirt embroidered "Stephanie."

Melody, 29, San Jose, Calif.

Sally's daughter is gifted. Sally talks forever about how she needs special challenges, regular schools aren't enough for her. She gets invited by universities to spend summers there. She also is a champion swimmer. Junior Olympics winner. And she plays the violin. I can't enter the conversation. My kids are normal. What can I say, "Tommy passed math"? "Susie can almost do her backstroke, and she plays chopsticks on the piano"? After I talk to her, I end up feeling like I've got the dullest kids on earth.

Janice, 42, San Jose, Calif.

Her daughter's so articulate, sophisticated, and manipulative, I have trouble remembering that she's only twelve. She flatters me, tells me I'm her mom's coolest friend. That I'm very cool for a grown-up. That I'm much skinnier than her mom. She asks my opinion on adult topics like the death penalty, legalization of drugs. Then, when she thinks I'm softened up, she asks me to persuade her mom to give her a bigger allowance. Or to give her permission to go to the mall with her friends. Or to let her see "R"-rated films. Whatever she wants at the moment. The girl's scary. Politicians could learn from her.

Chelsea, 35, Chicago, Ill.

She keeps no secrets from her kids. She talks about anything and everything right in front of them. Her son, Peter, was seven when he asked me, "Aunt Sherry, are you over your miscarriage yet?"

Sherry, 29, Salt Lake City, Utah

I knew her when we smoked pot all night and cut classes in high school. She lost her virginity in ninth grade. Now, she's ballistic when her teenagers want to go to the mall. She'd collapse if she found out they ever had a beer. She won't let them watch violent or sexy TV shows or see any movies that the church doesn't approve of. She'd go nuts if they ever cursed. Or if they ever found out *half* the stuff she did at their age.

Gina, 37, Elmira, N.Y.

Ellen works, so I just about raise her kids. They come to my house and eat out of my fridge. I'm at the market four times a day for juice and milk. I buy potato chips by the crate.

Erica, 40, Wexford, Pa.

At birthdays or Christmas, Amy gives our kids much more expensive presents than we can afford to give hers. I asked her to put a $10 limit on her gifts. She agreed, but didn't stick to it. She said she "couldn't resist" these fantastic Rollerblades or this huge boom box. I felt like a jerk handing her kids a couple of paperback books.

Brenda, 41, Cincinnati, Ohio

Her kids have every latest fad. CDs, computer, software and video games, hundreds of dollars' worth of sports equipment, a swimming pool, water slide, tree houses, electric cars, remote-control planes. Whenever they go there, my kids never want to come back to our house. "There's nothing to do here."

Julie, 43, Swarthmore, Pa.

She's always washing her children's hands. Scrubbing them with antibacterial soap. And she won't let them into certain parts of the house. Ever. Well, not that she lets *me* in either. I've never been in her living room. And I don't know anyone who has.

Veronica, 31, Los Angeles, Calif.

313

She means well, teaches her kids about causes. But she tends to see black and white, no grey. Wearing fur is wrong, but she has leather seats in her car. Animal research is wrong, but she uses medicines developed that way. She tells them to buy American-made products, but she wears imported clothes. Her kids eat fruit picked by underpaid farm workers. But she's got them fired up about the whales. They'd go to the mat to protect gorillas.

Emily, 38, Des Moines, Iowa

Hillary wants her son, who's sixteen, to date my fifteen-year-old daughter. She jokes about it, presses me to push it. My daughter thinks her son's a buffoon. She wouldn't shine her shoes with him. Meantime, Hillary's planning a wedding.

Clarice, 42, Toledo, Ohio

*M*argaret's daughter and my son are both thirteen, and they've played together since they were babies. Until Margaret teased them about how neat it would be if they got married. Now my son hides when they come over. If he sees their car pull up, he goes out the back door.

Liz, 39, Boulder, Colo.

*S*he reads their diaries, mail, goes through their pockets, their closets. Says she needs to know what's going on in their lives. I say, "Why don't you just ask them?"

She stares at me like I'm nuts. "Get real," she says. "Did you ever tell *your* mother anything?"

Jade, 35, Albuquerque, N.Mex.

She runs to school to yell at the teacher every time somebody calls little Stevie a nasty name. She calls the parents of kids he has fights with and yells at them. Not that Stevie doesn't need help. The kid cries for Mama if you look at him. She knows she's doing this—she even says, "You want to take on Stevie? Then you got to take on his Mama, too."

Melissa, 40, St. Louis, Mo.

Our girls are both twelve years old. And she has a way of bragging about her daughter at my daughter's expense. Like she'll talk about some boy's skating party. Then she'll gasp, "Wasn't your Suzi invited? *All* the kids are going."

Holly, 35, Bethesda, Md.

317

Simone says it's fine that our teenage daughters dress like tramps. Clunky heels and hot pants, ears pierced so much they'd set off metal detectors. Dyed hair. Fake fingernails. She tells me that this style is no big deal. That, before I fuss about it, I should think back to when I was a teen. "String bikinis? Day-glow body-painted birthday suits?"

Alexis, 45, Stamford, Conn.

She invites my kids places—to theme parks, movies, dinner, sleep-overs—without checking with me first, so I'm the bad guy if I say no. She says she's just spontaneous, that I'm too rigid and controlling.

Nikki, 36, St. Paul, Minn.

She took my teenagers bungee jumping. It was my fault, really. Because, before they left, I told her, no mixing with strangers. No pigging out on candy and junk food. No staying out late. But I did not specifically say, "No bungee jumping." Besides, it's not like she sent them to do it alone. She went, too. She figured that she'd better jump with them because if anything happened, she'd better be dead. At least she was right about something.

Alexis, 42, Boulder, Colo.

She has three children but has the urge to have more, which her husband doesn't. So whenever she feels like getting pregnant, she goes out and gets another animal. So far, she's got four cats, two canaries, a tankful of fish, a hermit crab, and a hamster. I suspect her husband's getting to the point where he'd go for the fourth child if she'd get rid of the zoo.

Edie, 32, Enid, Okla.

She makes her kids clean their plates. Every bite of food. Even peas. Even lima beans. *Meat loaf.* It's sickening. She's a complete fascist.

Paula, 27, Des Moines, Iowa

At her son's bar mitzvah, she sat me way off in a corner table with her ex-husband's elderly aunts. She told me she was two people short at the table and I was the only one she could count on to understand. I understand, all right. Wait till it's my son's turn. She'll need a telescope to see the head table.

Lynne, 34, Bala Cynwyd, Pa.

CHAPTER 9

DOWN TIME

There must be fifty ways to bash your buddy. Just disagree, Lee. Bicker and spat, Pat. Squabble and quibble, Cybil. And that's just to start. Because when nerves are frazzled and patience is thin, friends can go at each other at least as fiercely as the worst of enemies; after all, who's better equipped to hit the other's precise weak points, vulnerabilities, and sore spots?

Sooner or later, even the best of good buddies differ, argue, criticize, or correct. Their issues may be complex or simple, old or new, confronted or avoided, multiple or few. Their techniques may involve blunt shouting or subtle silence, callous cursing or sarcastic sweetness. Whether they are cool and aloof or swinging and swiping, friends occasionally need to vent their hostilities and clear the air.

"When we fight," Vera says, "it's usually because I'm down on myself. When I feel good about *me*, nothing she does bothers me. When I don't, all she has to do is blink and I want to kill her."

Whatever the reasons, when tensions build up, friends often release it onto each other. And many, secure that their relationships can take it, let go and say things that hurt, Gert. Or hang up the phone, Joan. Or cancel the plan, Jan. Or just count to ten, Jen. Because sooner or later, it'll pass.

She thinks compromise means letting others say their piece and then doing things her way. The woman *never* gives in. She just restates her idea more enthusiastically, as if it's new. Or as if it's the consensus.

Kathy, 34, Naples, Fla.

We've been friends since kindergarten and Nora never forgets anything I ever did to her. She's still mad that I broke her doll's head off when we were, like, seven. Or that I told her the wrong way to spell a word, so she lost the fifth-grade spelling bee. Or that I stole her boyfriend sophomore year. And junior year. I don't think she knows about Greg, the guy from senior year, or I'd still hear about that, too.

Cathy, 25, Boston, Mass.

She will not forgive me for the perm I gave her in high school. What's the big deal? It was nine years ago. And her hair grew back.

Adrian, 25, St. Louis, Mo.

325

Pam bears grudges, never moves on. She got mad when I bought myself the perfume she wore. This was like twenty years ago. She still remembers and won't tell me what perfume she wears now, tells me she has to order it specially from an importer, so I might as well forget it. Like I care.

Debbie, 39, Braintree, Mass.

Jane teases me about my temper. She's amused when I lose it, goads me on. We were waiting at a department store counter when someone else strolled up and the saleswoman went right over to her and said, "Can I help you?" Jane elbowed me and grinned, "Go on, Midge. Tell her who you are!"

Midge, 39, Folcroft, Pa.

I will never forgive her for making me wear that taxicab-yellow bridesmaid gown. It was March—I was pale and sallow and looked almost as yellow as the dress. Her wedding pictures captured the skin tones perfectly. The worst part was that all the other brides-maids wore softer, golden shades. She said she wanted me to stand out.

Michelle, 24, Kenosha, Wis.

Arguing isn't Bea's thing. She doesn't bother with words. She gives dirty looks that make you want to crawl into some swampy hole, looks that make you think you'd be at home in a spittoon.

Agatha, 29, Corpus Christi, Tex.

327

onna and I were roommates in college and had a huge fight—I mean *huge*—over a can of tuna fish. I'd bought it because I *knew* I'd be hungry in the middle of the night while cramming for exams. So about three in the morning, I go to fix myself a sandwich and, guess what, she'd eaten it. She didn't ask, "Do you mind if I eat your tuna?" Didn't even offer, "Want half a sandwich? I'm making tuna." She didn't say a word. She just helped herself to something that wasn't hers and *ate* it. The empty can was in the trash. I'm still mad about this. Anyhow, I just turned fifty. I get a package in the mail. But she sent the kind in *oil*. She knows I'd never eat tuna in oil. *My* can was in spring water.

Selena, 50, St. Louis, Mo.

arlene will not argue. Will not discuss a topic you don't agree on. If there's a conflict, she says, "That's okay," raises an eyebrow, and gives you the silent treatment. You'll be in the middle of a conversation and she suddenly gets busy reading a magazine or studying a hangnail. It gets chilly in the room. Depending on the importance of the topic, this can go on for hours or days.

Holly, 33, Stamford, Conn.

don't dare argue with Marilyn. If I get her too mad, she might tell my mother that I smoke.

Carlee, 35, Shreveport, La.

She does not listen to anything negative. Criticism bounces off of her like Flubber. She simply dismisses what she doesn't want to hear, lets it float past her into the cosmos. Even if you insult her, she's smiling, unperturbed. So when you're mad at her, you might as well not waste your voice. She'll only make you madder.

Cheryl, 33, Lexington, Ky.

Her voice is normally high. When she gets excited or mad, it gets higher and higher until you think she's going to fly away.

Katie, 31, Des Moines, Iowa

Mara thinks PMS gives her a license to kill. Nobody else has this right, just her. She's guiltless; later, she feels no need to apologize for anything she's said or done. It wasn't her fault. It was PMS.

Mandy, 21, Boca Raton, Fla.

When she's mad, she gets real animated and doesn't take time to swallow. Sprays spit all over the place.

Shelby, 22, Orlando, Fla.

I can predict what she'll say, her tone of voice, her exact words. I know which tune she'll hum. The complaint she'll make. I know when she thinks the weather's too hot or too cold or too dry or too wet. And I don't want to hear it. She's dear. I love her and would do anything for her. But sometimes I have to get away from her or—so help me—I'd kill her.

Brandy, 28, Nashville, Tenn.

Helen'll yell at a waiter because her steak was too well done or she had to wait too long for a glass of wine. She'll call him a lazy idiot, an incompetent imbecile, and storm out. And either I go with her, as if I support her terrible tantrum, or I'm left sitting there alone facing the person she's just reamed. Like, "I hardly know her. She actually just happened to sit at my table—it was very odd. Please don't spit in my coffee."

Loni, 33, Kenosha, Wis.

Julia fights to kill, holds back nothing. I've seen her decimate people, tell them what she thinks of them and leave them cut to the bone. When she's irritated, I tread lightly.

Ellyn, 25, Providence, R.I.

333

Rhonda never feels the urge to apologize. Whatever mood she's in is what everyone else has to deal with. She can cancel plans, ignore you, pick fights, call names. Whatever. If she's upset, the world can go to hell. She expects unconditional, permanent love.

Leah, 31, Denver, Colo.

Sonia will never admit she was wrong. Instead, she gets real sweet, goes overboard to please you. Drives carpool on your day, calls to see if you need anything at the grocery. Leaves you cheery messages on your voice mail.

Lorraine, 41, Ames, Iowa

June cannot be wrong. Ever. She might change her mind. Might revise her opinion. But she's not wrong. The store's distorted lighting made that lilac suit look good on her. The sunblock bottle never warned that lips can burn. The driver in front of her put her brakes on too fast. All evidence to the contrary is misleading; she's always right.

Melanie, 32, Washington, D.C.

My husband and I are atheists and this upsets her, so she took our kids to a minister and had them baptized secretly. We didn't talk for a week after that, but then I figured, if there is no God, what difference does it make, and if there *is*, then it couldn't hurt.

Blanche, 36, Little Rock, Ark.

335

When she's mad, Gabbey snaps. Explodes. Rips you apart and then, poof, she's immediately over it. It's out of her system. She's sunny and cheerful again, and can't imagine why you're upset.

Paula, 27, Jackson Hole, Wyo.

We go to lunch, talk on the phone, take day trips the way women do when they have time. We hang out together. She bakes me banana bread. But she will *not* give me the name of her handyman. For years, I've asked for it and she says, "No." Just plain, flat, "No." This is a longstanding issue between us. He does great work for her, and I'd like him to help me out, too. One day, I'll kidnap him as he arrives at her house. I'll hide in the bushes, wait for him, and pounce. Or I'll wait till he's leaving her place and follow him home. She'd die.

Lois, 44, Bethesda, Md.

Lorraine gets involved in other people's business. She walks right into arguments between me and my husband and takes his side, adds her two cents. She starts on me for picking on him, puts her arm on his shoulder and says, "Leave the poor guy alone, Laurie. Stop dumping on him. You treat him like dog food."

Stephanie, 41, Chevy Chase, Md.

When we disagree, she tells me how difficult I am to put up with and how lucky I am that she's my friend because nobody else would put up with me. If I tell her to get lost, she says, "See what I mean? No one else would stick around after being talked to like that."

Reggie, 26, St. Paul, Minn.

nnie is five foot two—maybe. I'm five foot nine. But, if she's p.o.'d she will take on anyone, big or small. Me included. She doesn't care about facts. Right and wrong are irrelevant. If she feels like going at it, we go at it. And she's brutal, brings out the absolute worst in me. She'll say anything, and so will I, until one of us starts laughing at how outrageous we are and the whole explosion giggles itself away.

Veronica, 22, Long Island, N.Y.

know she's mad when she starts calling me "Honey," or "Dear." She knows this'll make *me* mad. So, we're off.

J.J., 27, San Antonio, Tex.

339

When she's in a bad mood, she bickers. Whatever I say or do is wrong. Not a lot wrong. Just a teeny tiny little bit wrong. And she can't let it pass; she *has* to correct every teeny tiny little point, clarify every itsy-bitsy detail. We're like an old married couple. But, actually, she's much worse than my husband; he doesn't notice what I say or do, much less correct it.

Virginia, 37, Norfolk, Conn.

When we have a fight, she takes to her bed. Says she has a migraine. Won't answer the phone for three days.

Norma Jean, 41, Selma, Ala.

340

When she's mad, she doesn't say so or discuss it intelligently. She's not that direct. Instead, she disagrees with me about every little thing. If I say it's noon, she says, "No, it's three minutes after." If I say something's white, she says, "No, it's eggshell." If I say it's a hundred degrees outside, she says, "No, it's ninety-nine."

Natalie, 27, Sacramento, Calif.

We agree about nothing. Not politics, not abortion, not religion. We don't usually like the same movies, TV shows, music, or restaurants, and we don't enjoy the same books. We've argued about everything as long as we've known each other. The only thing we agree on is that we like each other.

Margaret, 49, Aurora, Ill.

We suffer from the "too many cooks" syndrome. Liz has to do things her way; I have to do things mine. Neither one can compromise, so we clash. The choice is my way or hers. Kill or be killed.

Chloe, 42, Green Bay, Wis.

e're both very intense, can exhaust each other. So we get together, then back off for a few weeks. It's fine. It's our pattern. We're so alike in temperament that we can be compatible only about half the time.

Valerie, 39, West Chester, Pa.

There are actually years when we just aren't in the mood for each other. Maybe we get too involved, get our identities tangled up. Maybe we get too close. Competitive. I don't know. Just, once in a while, with no fight or formality, she's gone her way, and I've gone mine. Nothing's said. We're not mad. We just don't get together again for a while. Then, again without fanfare, we do, and pick up where we left off. I have no idea why. Rhythm? Tides? Astrological compatibility? Karma?

Eve, 46, Alexandria, Va.

Barb accuses me of expressing my anger indirectly by being late for a lunch date or forgetting something she's asked me to do, like copying a recipe or returning a book to the library. She says I do these things on purpose to express my deep-seated feelings of hostility. I say, "Oops. Sorry." But I can't talk directly about why I'm angry at her because, until she tells me, I have no idea that I am.

Rachel, 33, Olean, N.Y.

She never says she's been wrong. She says, "I'm sorry you feel that way." As if *I'm* at fault for being upset by something she's done.

MaryJane, 36, Saginaw, Mich.

345

When we're mad, for whatever reason, we don't talk to each other. We're both stubborn, and neither one will give in and be the first to call. This can go on for days. Weeks. We have to bump into each other on mutual ground, like church or the grocery store, to resume contact. Sometimes I have to shop four times a day to bump into her, though.

Iris, 40, Manchester, N.H.

She tries to soothe me when I'm mad at her. She says she understands, sees my point of view, supports my feelings, forgives my irrational behavior, accepts me with all my faults. She smiles sweetly. I want to kill her. But she'd just nod tolerantly, and forgive that, too.

346

Paige, 30, Lubbock, Tex.

W hen I stand up for my rights, Suzanne gets gone, like she doesn't know me. If someone cuts in line in front of me and I say, "I believe I was here first." Or if I ask to see a restaurant manager because service is bad. Or if I just want to politely register a complaint anywhere about anything, she's gone. Even when I'm right beyond the shadow of a doubt. She's terrified I'm going to "create a scene." She prefers to roll over and play dead.

Tess, 41, Miami, Fla.

THICK AND THIN

No matter what else we have to say about them, our friends are with us in good times and bad. Even if they have bad hair or bad habits, underpay tips or overrate men, come late to lunch or call too much, they are there, with us, through the course of our lives. We have memories in common. When we're with them, we feel familiar, comfortable, accepted. We don't need to prove ourselves. We affirm each other's worth, validate each other's existences. As we journey through life's stages and changes, traveling parallel paths through uncharted turf, we are reassured by keeping each other in sight. And, as we progress from young girls to old women, we create our own territory, safe, exclusive, timeless, inhabited by nostalgia, and built on bonds no one can break.

After I spend time with her, I'm cheered up. My job seems not so dull, my husband not so tuned-out, my kids not so impossible. My house seems not so messy. Compared to hers, my life seems peachy.

Jan, 40, Dallas, Tex.

Helen's kids are grown and she's not doing well with her empty nest. She spends all her time anticipating old age and doing projects like revising her will, selling most of her furniture—all in preparation for checking out. She wants me to visit retirement communities with her and make reservations. She bought herself a rocking chair, saying, "I'd better get what I'll need now, because when I need it, I won't be able to." I swear, for her birthday, I'm sending her a walker.

Ruth, 61, Portland, Maine

351

The woman will not let me tell a story without stopping me and correcting me, and changing the whole subject. She makes me sound like a liar, catching me up on details that have no importance whatsoever. Like, I'll start to talk about an accident that happened about ten years ago. She'll jump right in and say, "Mary, it was fourteen years ago. I know because it was the same year I went to Georgia. . . ." And before you know it, she's talking about her trip to Savannah. If I start up again, she finds some other hole in my story and does the same thing.

Mary, 67, Little Rock, Ark.

Amy and I have been close since high school. We were in the same crowd, dated the same guys—sometimes at the same time. So, over the years, the two of us have developed our own private sphere of memories. Nobody else gets our private jokes, or makes sense out of the references we make to the past. She's godmother to my son. I know her so well, I'd trust her with my life. But not—after what happened in high school—with my husband.

Rebecca, 35, Cambridge, Mass.

She laughs at my jokes. Even when no one else does. For this alone, she has my undying friendship.

Meg, 37, Dayton, Ohio

When I saw her at the airport for the first time in nine years, she ran up and hugged me. I pushed her away, held her at arms length so I could see her. She got all upset and insulted because she thought I was pushing her away. She didn't understand that I simply couldn't *see* her if she stood too close: My eyesight isn't what it used to be. But, given how we've both changed, that's just as well.

Renee, 61, Sarasota, Fla.

She told me I had fear of success and kept bugging me until I went back to finish school and get my degree. You'd have thought it was her diploma, the way she cried.

Laurie, 31, Fort Myers, Fla.

We met in high school. Her parents would've killed her if they found out she smoked, so when her mom walked in unexpectedly, she shoved her cigarette into my hand. Her mother called my mother, and I got in trouble, instead. It was always like that. I covered for her, took the blame to protect her. Now, she's convinced herself that everything was the other way around. She claims she was an angel, that she kept *me* from getting thrown out of school. She actually insists that that was *my* cigarette.

Cindy, 31, Columbus, Ohio

ver the years, we've developed our own code words, symbols that no one else can understand. For example, we don't say something is "smooth." We say it's an "Eddie Doyle," because I walked in on them once, when we were roommates, and an instant legend was born—nothing in this world, I mean *nothing*, will ever be as sleek as that boy's backside. Mmmm mmm.

Yvonne, 31, Houston, Tex.

She and her husband bought cemetery plots neighboring ours. We're together for eternity. My husband's angry about this, says that, with the two of us around, he won't ever get any peace.

Margie, 43, Boise, Idaho

357

Every few years, she decides to reinvent herself. This means she travels, learns a new language, goes back to school, loses weight, kicks out the current man in her life, drops her present friends. After a few months, she resurfaces, supposedly to show off her new persona. I try to act impressed. And, for a few days, I don't let myself finish her sentences for her.

Phoebe, 37, Wilmington, Del.

My best friend died in a car accident when she was just twenty. I think of her every day. And, when I goof up, I still hear her sarcastic comments. I miss her. It's been nine years, and she's still my best friend. Always will be.

Patsy, 29, Pasadena, Calif.

Every year, we get together for a long weekend. With her, I resurrect the person I was before kids, husband, bills, careers, responsibilities, stretch marks. We don't have to talk about the past; it's there, mixed in with the present. Our memories are in our jokes, and the way we act with each other. We bring out parts of ourselves that our husbands and kids aren't aware of, have no use for, and will never know. When we get together, the girls we used to be get a chance to howl.

Barb, 36, Shaker Heights, Ohio

've always strived for her approval, even though I know this is a futile task. It's not what she says; it's what she doesn't say. She'll say, "Oh, you got your hair cut." Her tone is completely flat, not enthusiastic, not disgusted. Nothing. She won't give you the satisfaction of an opinion. Won't say, "Gee. You look great." Or, "Ohmygod! You look awful." She just states a fact. If you ask what she thinks of it, she'll say, "It's what *you* think that counts. Do *you* like it?" I've considered violence.

Carson, 42, New York, N.Y.

When my daughter got her driver's license, Gail sent e-mail, "Don't worry. Lightning doesn't strike twice." Because when I got my license, she and I went for a ride to celebrate and I totaled my mom's car. Gail sees things in context. She knows what things mean to me, in a way no one else does. We share that long view, for better or worse.

Camille, 43, Darien, Conn.

She makes stuff up, remembers things that never happened. She doesn't just embellish history; she invents it. As if I don't know the truth. As if I'd believe she was the homecoming queen. As if I wasn't there. As if I don't know she was lucky to get a *date*.

Sandie, 36, Minneapolis, Minn.

361

We diet together. Perpetually. Between the two of us, over the years, we've lost about a thousand pounds. Never mind how much we've gained.

Penny, 38, Lynchburg, Va.

ost of my family's a thousand miles away, so Rozzy has us over every holiday, along with all her cousins, uncles, nephews, nieces, and in-laws. We're part of her family. We know this because we're included in the squabbling, complaining, hollering, and scolding. And she assigns us jobs, like she's a boot camp sergeant. "Make a salad, Della. Make drinks, Al. Carve the turkey. Serve the soup. Sit down. Be quiet. Say grace. Eat."

Della, 40, Los Angeles, Calif.

Lovers you can break up with, and husbands
you can divorce. But friends—well, friends are tougher
to get rid of. Jeannie won't let me alone, won't let
me kiss her off. She's determined that good friends
stick by you, and she reads my solitude as isolation,
contemplation as depression. When I tell her to
leave me alone, she hears it as a desperate cry for
companionship.

Hannah, 30, Boston, Mass.

In our wills, should we both die, my husband and I have named Sarah guardian of our child. She and her husband named us guardian of hers. We *pray* that she lives to a ripe old age—she has four kids and they're all monsters. Still, who you'd entrust your kids to—that says it all, doesn't it?

Robyn, 31, Nyack, N.Y.

e met when our kids were in kindergarten.
I seriously don't know how I managed before. Suzi
shares information about inexpensive vacation spots,
bargains, discount stores, camps, karate lessons, diets,
recipes. She introduced me to people at the elemen-
tary school. She listens to me when my husband won't
or can't anymore. She makes me laugh when I'm
strung out, or makes me remember that, even if I can't
laugh now, I will someday. That these are the good
old days.

Marian, 29, Southfield, Mich.

Donna and I drove our kids to the overnight camp we used to go to. We dropped them off by the same bunks we slept in. The air felt the same, smelled the same. We stood at the lake, looking at each other. Our eyes filled with tears and we hugged. Words were useless. What was there to say? There were no words.

Carolyn, 35, Jenkintown, Pa.

For my fortieth birthday, she helped my husband give me a surprise party. She provided and blew up every unflattering photograph ever taken of me. Poster-sized pictures, all over the room, treated my friends to visions of me before I had braces, *while* I had them, before my nose was fixed, with bad hair, with half-closed eyes. But, see, that was dumb: She's going to be forty in a year, four months, and eight days. What could she have been thinking?

Rita, 40, Omaha, Nebr.

Stella has stood with me in amazement at every phase of life. She helps me appreciate the full implication, the meaning of whatever's happening—whether it's being able to go to the movies ourselves, being allowed to wear lipstick and high heels, going to the prom, or getting married. All our lives, we've looked at each other and said, "Can you believe this is *happening*?" Pregnancies, babies, divorces—whatever stage we're at, we're always amazed. In a few more years, we'll look at each other and say, "Can you believe this is happening? Us? In the *home*?"

Seema, 52, Cleveland, Ohio

knew her when she was a brunette. In fact, I took part in her very first peroxide episode. It turned the front half of her hair bright orange. We've been friends through large and little noses, fat and skinny thighs, thick and thin waists. She has to be nice to me: I have the photos *and* the negatives.

Ruth, 43, Telluride, Colo.

She tells me she can't afford to lose me; I'm the only one still alive besides her who remembers Puggsie, her first dog.

Rebecca, 46, Fort Worth, Tex.

We live three thousand miles apart, so we take a few days every year and meet at a halfway point. She's my vitamin. My elixir. I come back refreshed, with a new perspective. She stimulates me by expecting me to be the person she thinks I am. She sees the best in me, inspires me to be my best. When I'm with her, I like me. When she smiles and confides in me, I think: I must be a person worth knowing.

Grace, 41, Seattle, Wash.

I have no idea what my husband sees when he looks at me. Or why he loves me. Genders are blind to each other; sexuality makes for distortions. Something prevents him from seeing my spider veins and grey roots. But, Lord knows, Jenny sees it all and loves me anyway. My husband's my life partner and we share all our worldly goods, our kids. I love him. But my best, most satisfying laughs, my feelings of being most appreciated as a person, for who I am, are with Jenny.

Gwen, 43, Austin, Tex.